W9-BLU-519
CANADA
THE NORTHEAST
pages 12–35
THE MIDWEST
pages 62–87
THE WEST
pages 98–121
THE SOUTHEAST
pages 36–61
THE SOUTHWEST
pages 88–97
ATLANTIC OCEAN
GULF OF MEXICO
BAHAMAS
CUBA
MEXICO
100°W
80°W
60°W
20°W
40°N
20°N
120°W

NATIONAL GEOGRAPHIC KIDS
BEGINNER'S UNITED STATES ATLAS
NATIONAL GEOGRAPHIC
WASHINGTON, D.C.

Table of Contents

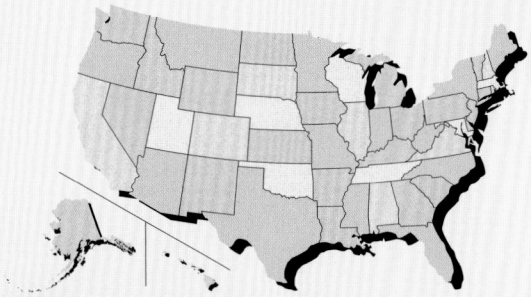

4 Learning the Basics

What Is a Map? 4
The Physical United States 6
The Political United States 8
The District of Columbia 10

12 The Northeast

Connecticut 14
Delaware 16
Maine 18
Maryland 20
Massachusetts 22
New Hampshire 24
New Jersey 26
New York 28
Pennsylvania 30
Rhode Island 32
Vermont 34

36 The Southeast

Alabama 38
Arkansas 40
Florida 42
Georgia 44
Kentucky 46
Louisiana 48
Mississippi 50
North Carolina 52
South Carolina 54
Tennessee 56
Virginia 58
West Virginia 60

62 The Midwest

Illinois **64**
Indiana **66**
Iowa **68**
Kansas **70**
Michigan **72**
Minnesota **74**
Missouri **76**
Nebraska **78**
North Dakota **80**
Ohio **82**
South Dakota **84**
Wisconsin **86**

98 The West

Alaska **100**
California **102**
Colorado **104**
Hawai'i **106**
Idaho **108**
Montana **110**
Nevada **112**
Oregon **114**
Utah **116**
Washington **118**
Wyoming **120**

122 The Territories

Political Map and
Fact Boxes **122**

88 The Southwest

Arizona **90**
New Mexico **92**
Oklahoma **94**
Texas **96**

124 The United States at a Glance **124**

Glossary **125**
Index **126**
Two-Letter Postal Codes **127**
Credits **128**

What Is a Map?

An atlas is a collection of maps and pictures. A map is a drawing of a place as it looks from above. It is flat, and it is smaller than the place it shows. Learning to read a map can help you find where you are and where you want to go. **Mapping your home ...**

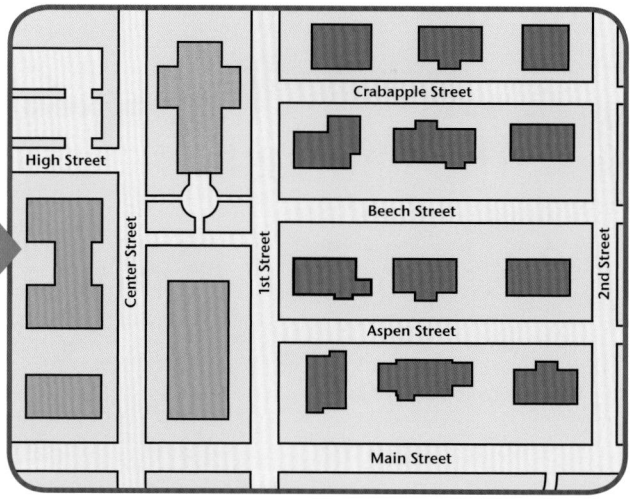

From a bird's-eye view ...
If you were a bird flying directly overhead, you would see only the tops of things. You wouldn't see walls, tree trunks, tires, or feet.

On a large-scale map ... you see places from a bird's-eye view. But a map uses drawings called symbols to show things on the ground, such as houses or streets. The map of the National Mall in Washington, D.C., on pages 10–11 is an example of a large-scale map.

Finding places on the map

A **map** can help you get where you want to go. A map helps you read it by showing you north, south, east, and west, plus a key and a scale.

→ A **compass rose** helps you travel in the right direction. It tells you where north (N), south (S), east (E), and west (W) are on your map. Often only a north arrow is used.

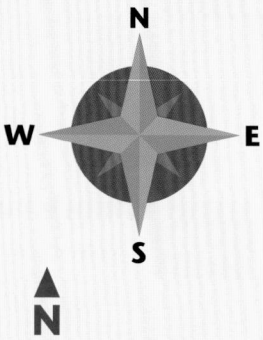

→ A **map key** helps you understand the symbols used by the mapmaker to show things like buildings, towns, or rivers on the map.

- ★ State capital
- •• City or town
- ■ Point of interest
- ---- National trail
- •••• Country boundary
- ····· State boundary
- Indian Reservation
- State Park
- National Park Service
- National Forest land

0 — 100 miles
0 — 100 kilometers

← A **scale** tells you about distance on a map. The scale shows what length on the map represents the labeled distance on the ground.

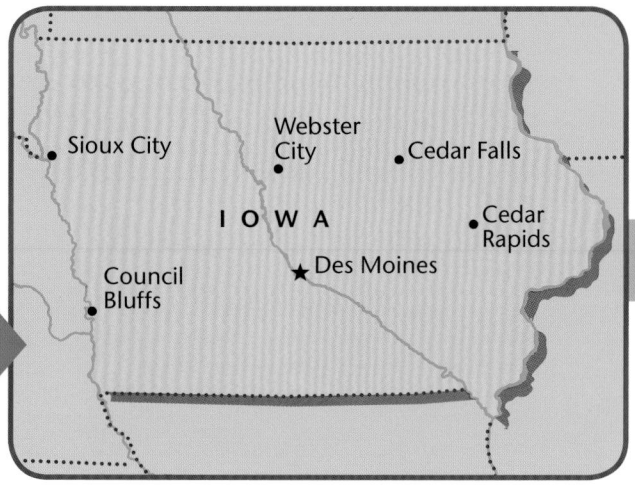

On an intermediate-scale map ... you see a place from much higher up. A town appears as a tiny dot. You can't see houses, but you can see more of the land around the town. Most maps in this atlas show a whole state with its towns and other special features.

On a small-scale map ... you can see much more of the country around a state, including other states. But on a small-scale map there is much less detail. You can no longer see most features within the state. Two states—Alaska and Hawai'i—are often shown in separate boxes or on a map of the whole continent, as on pages 6–7.

Map Key for the State Maps in This Atlas

- Aspen .....*town of under 25,000 residents*
- Frankfort .....*town of 25,000 to 99,999*
- San Jose .....*city of 100,000 to 999,999*
- New York .....*city of 1,000,000 and over*

National capital
State capital
Pass
Point of interest
High point
Low point
River
Intermittent river
Canal
Bridge
National trail
Country boundary
State boundary
Continental Divide
Lake
Intermittent lake

Dry lake
Swamp
Glacier
Sand
Lava
Area below sea level
Indian Reservation (I.R.)
State Park (S.P.)
National Park Service
National Historical Park (N.H.P.)
National Lakeshore
National Marine Sanctuary (N.M.S.)
National Monument (NAT. MON.)
National Park (N.P.)
National Preserve (N. PRES.)
National Recreation Area (N.R.A.)
National River
National Scenic Area
National Seashore
National Volcanic Monument
National Forest land
National Grassland (N.G.)

The Land

Land regions The rugged Sierra Nevada and Rocky Mountains run north to south through the western United States. Between these mountains are dry lands with little vegetation. East of the Rockies are wide, grassy plains and the older, lower Appalachian Mountains.

Water The Mississippi–Missouri is the longest river system in the United States. The Great Lakes are the largest freshwater lakes in the country.

Climate The United States has many climate types—from cold Alaska to tropical Hawai'i, with milder climates in the other 48 states.

Plants The United States has forests where there is plenty of rain. Grasslands cover drier areas.

Animals There are many kinds of animals—everything from bears and deer to songbirds large and small.

← North America is famous for its **deciduous forests.** Leaves turn fiery colors each fall.

↑ Waves off the Pacific Ocean roll onto a beach along the shore of Moloka'i, one of the islands that make up the state of **Hawai'i.**

Hawaii

← The majestic bald eagle is the national bird of the United States. It is found throughout the country, but about half live in **Alaska.**

↓ Deserts are found in the southwestern part of the United States. This large rock formation, called the Mitten, is in **Monument Valley** in Utah.

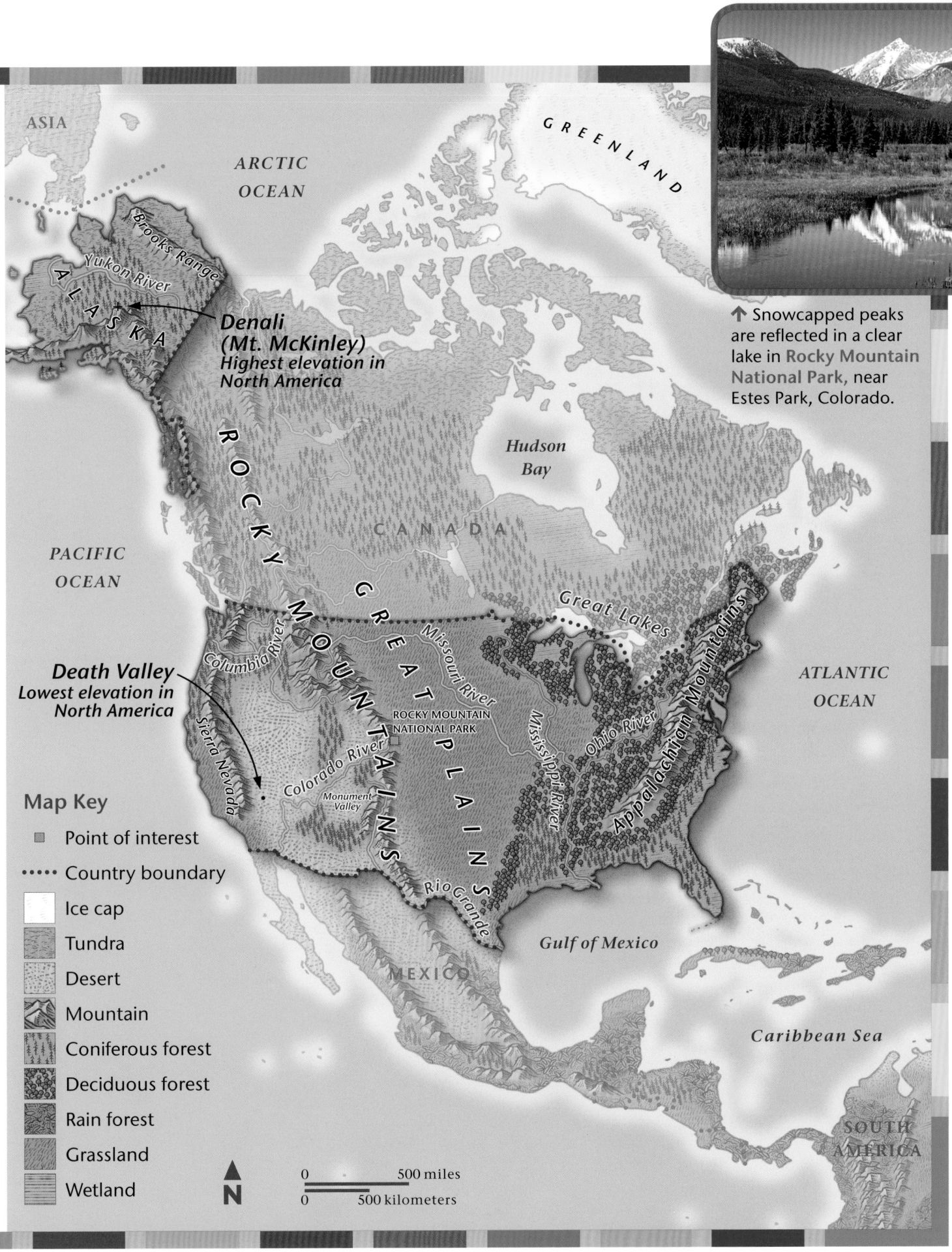

↑ Snowcapped peaks are reflected in a clear lake in **Rocky Mountain National Park**, near Estes Park, Colorado.

The People

States The United States is made up of 50 states. Alaska and Hawai'i are separated from the rest of the country. So you can see them close up, they are shown in the Pacific Ocean south of California.

Cities Washington, D.C., is the national capital. Each state also has a capital city. New York City has the most people.

People The United States is made up of people from almost every country in the world. Most live and work in and around cities.

Languages English is the main language, followed by Spanish.

Products The main products include cars, machinery, petroleum, natural gas, coal, beef, wheat, and forest products.

↑ Chinese New Year is a big celebration in San Francisco. Many Chinese Americans live in this California city.

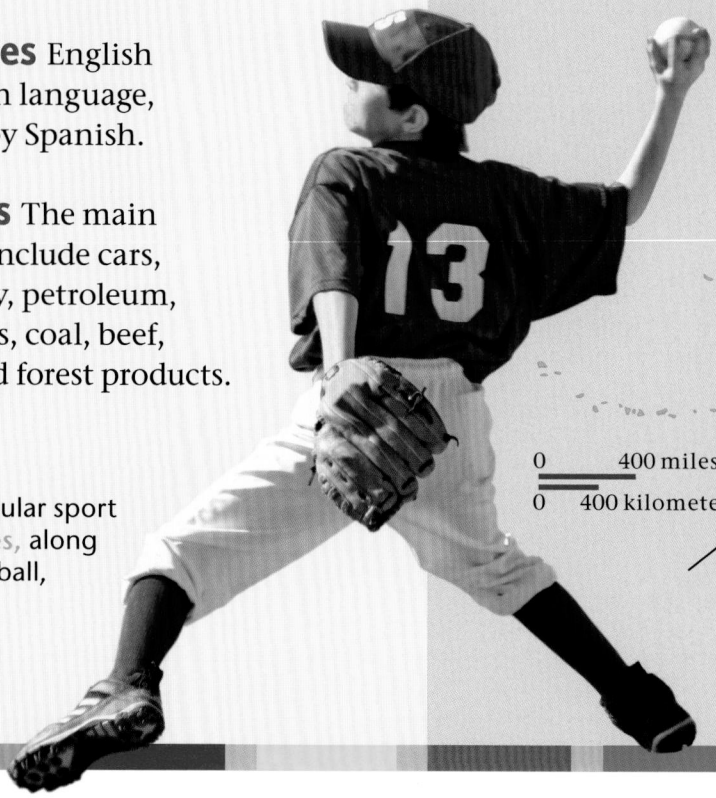

→ Baseball is a popular sport in the United States, along with soccer, basketball, and football.

Columbia River
Seattle
Olympia
WASHINGTON
Portland
Salem
OREGON
IDAHO
Boise
CALIFORNIA
Sacramento
Carson City
NEVADA
Salt Lake City
UT
San Francisco
San Jose
Las Vegas
ARIZO
Los Angeles
Phoenix
San Diego
Tucson
PACIFIC OCEAN
ALASKA
Juneau
0 400 miles
0 400 kilometers
HAWAI'I
Honolulu
0 150 miles
0 150 kilometers

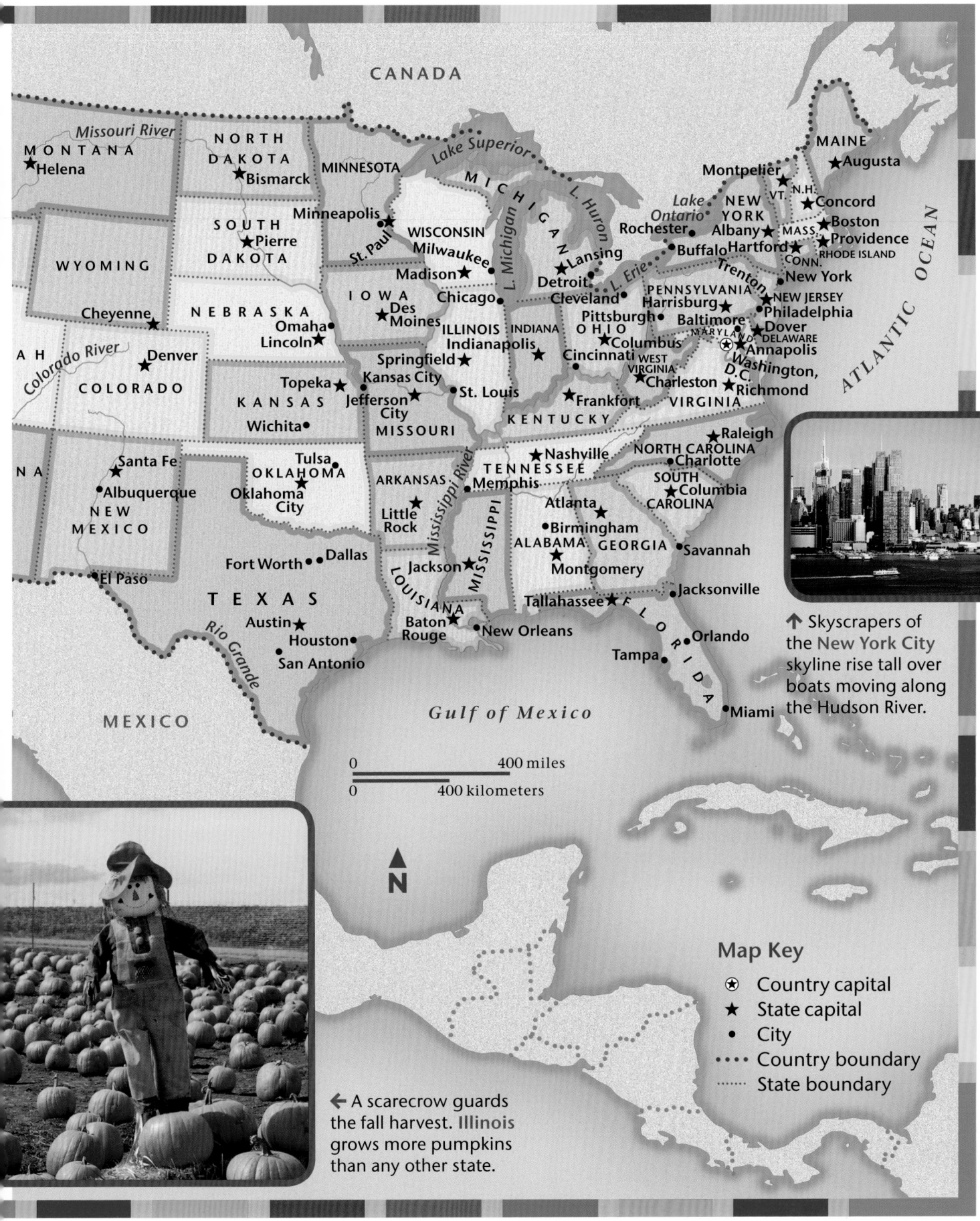

↑ Skyscrapers of the New York City skyline rise tall over boats moving along the Hudson River.

← A scarecrow guards the fall harvest. Illinois grows more pumpkins than any other state.

The National Capital: Washington, D.C.

Land & Water The National Mall, the Potomac River, and the Anacostia River are important land and water features of the District of Columbia.

Statehood The District of Columbia was founded in 1790, but it is not a state.

People & Places The District of Columbia's population is 672,228. Known as Washington, D.C., the city is the seat of the U.S. government.

Fun Fact The flag of the District of Columbia, with three red stars and two red stripes, is based on the shield in George Washington's family coat of arms.

Washington, D.C. Flag

American Beauty Rose
Official Flower

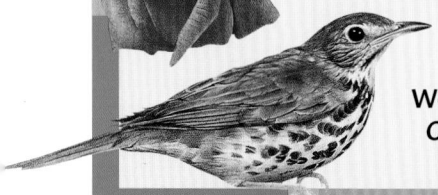

Wood Thrush
Official Bird

→ The **Smithsonian Institution**, the world's largest museum, is actually made up of 19 museums and the National Zoo. Established in 1846, it is sometimes called the nation's attic because of its large collections.

← **Abraham Lincoln,** who was president during the Civil War and a strong opponent of slavery, is remembered in a memorial that houses this seated statue at the west end of the National Mall.

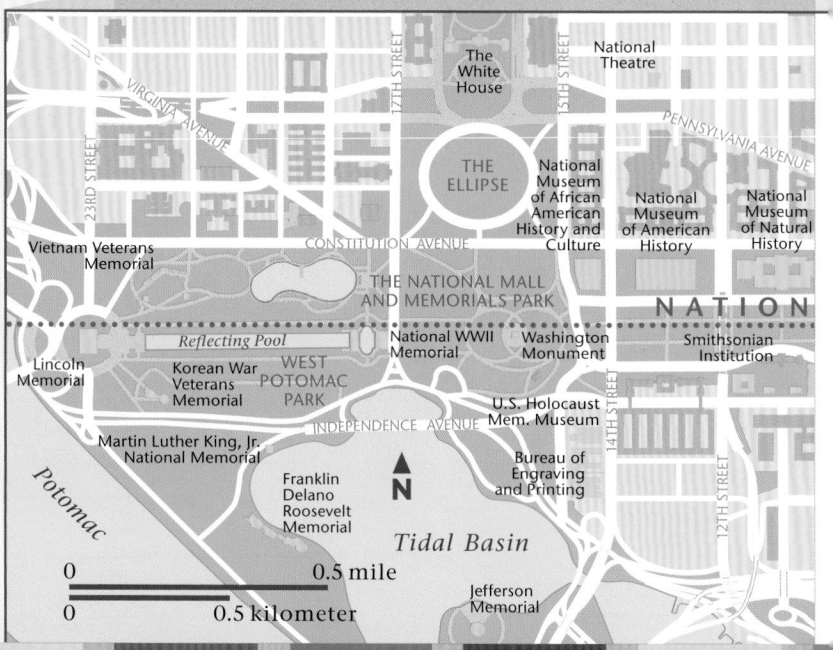

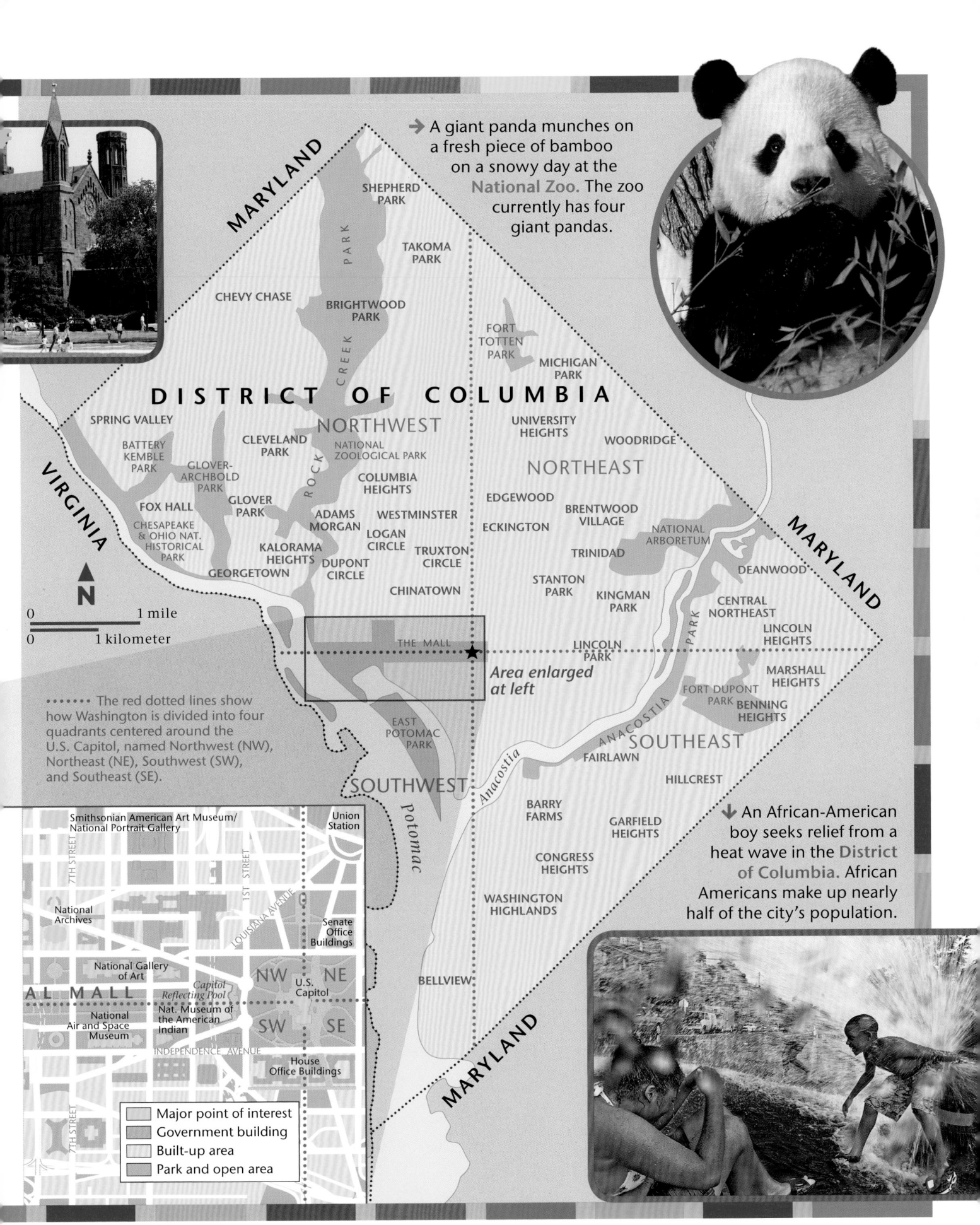

→ A giant panda munches on a fresh piece of bamboo on a snowy day at the **National Zoo.** The zoo currently has four giant pandas.

↓ An African-American boy seeks relief from a heat wave in the **District of Columbia.** African Americans make up nearly half of the city's population.

····· The red dotted lines show how Washington is divided into four quadrants centered around the U.S. Capitol, named Northwest (NW), Northeast (NE), Southwest (SW), and Southeast (SE).

The Northeast

Early settlers and traders from Europe established colonies in the Northeast region. These colonies eventually became states. Over time, people came from countries all around the world to live in the United States. Many of these people arrived through large port cities in the Northeast, including New York City, NY, Boston, MA, and Baltimore, MD. They brought with them different customs, languages, and beliefs that make the Northeast a region of great variety. Today the Northeast region includes the country's financial center, New York City, and its political capital, Washington, D.C.

Water plunges as much as 110 feet (34 m) over the American Falls on the Niagara River near New York's northwestern border with our neighbor Canada. Black bears are common in the forests of the region.

Connecticut

Land & Water Mount Frissell, the Connecticut River, and Long Island Sound are important land and water features of Connecticut.

Statehood Connecticut became the 5th state in 1788.

People & Places Connecticut's population is 3,590,886. Hartford is the state capital. The largest city is Bridgeport.

Fun Fact The sperm whale, Connecticut's state animal, is known for its massive head. Its brain is larger than that of any other creature known to have lived on Earth.

↑ Girls' lacrosse is popular in schools and colleges in **Connecticut** and across the United States. It was adapted from a Native American game.

Connecticut State Flag

Mountain Laurel
State Flower

Robin
State Bird

← The *Charles W. Morgan,* launched in 1841 and now docked in **Mystic Seaport,** is the only remaining wooden whaling ship in the world.

MASSACHUSETTS
Canaan
Highest point in Connecticut
Enfield
Barkhamsted Reservoir
Connecticut
Putnam
Farmington
RHODE ISLAND
Torrington
Hartford ★
Manchester
Newington
Bristol
New Britain
CONNECTICUT
Waterbury
Middletown
Meriden
Norwich
Gardner Lake
Thames
MASHANTUCKET PEQUOT I.R.
Connecticut
North Haven
Housatonic
Lake Gaillard
New London
Groton
Mystic
New Haven
East Haven
West Haven
BLOCK ISLAND SOUND
Bridgeport
NEW YORK
LONG ISLAND SOUND
0 20 miles
0 20 kilometers

Map Key

★ State capital
●●● City or town
····· State boundary
- - - - National trail
Indian Reservation
State Park

N

← The town of **Waterbury** was founded more than 300 years ago. Factories that made brass products earned the town the nickname "Brass City."

Delaware

Land & Water The Barrier Islands, Cypress Swamp, and Delaware Bay are important land and water features of Delaware.

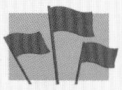

Statehood Delaware became the 1st state in 1787.

People & Places Delaware's population is 945,934. Dover is the state capital. The largest city is Wilmington.

Fun Fact Each year contestants bring pumpkins and launching machines to the Punkin Chunkin World Championship in Bridgeville to see who can toss their big orange squash the farthest.

↑ The Delmarva Peninsula, with more than 1,500 poultry growers, is a major producing area for chickens. The industry's trade association is located in **Georgetown**.

→ Patriotic boys wave American flags at a Delaware motorsports track near **Delmar**. Racing fans have come to the tracks since they opened in 1963.

↓ Brightly colored umbrellas dot **Bethany Beach**. Sun, sand, and surf attract thousands of vacationers each year to Delaware's shore.

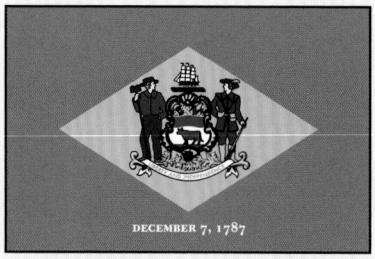

Delaware State Flag

Peach Blossom
State Flower

Blue Hen Chicken
State Bird

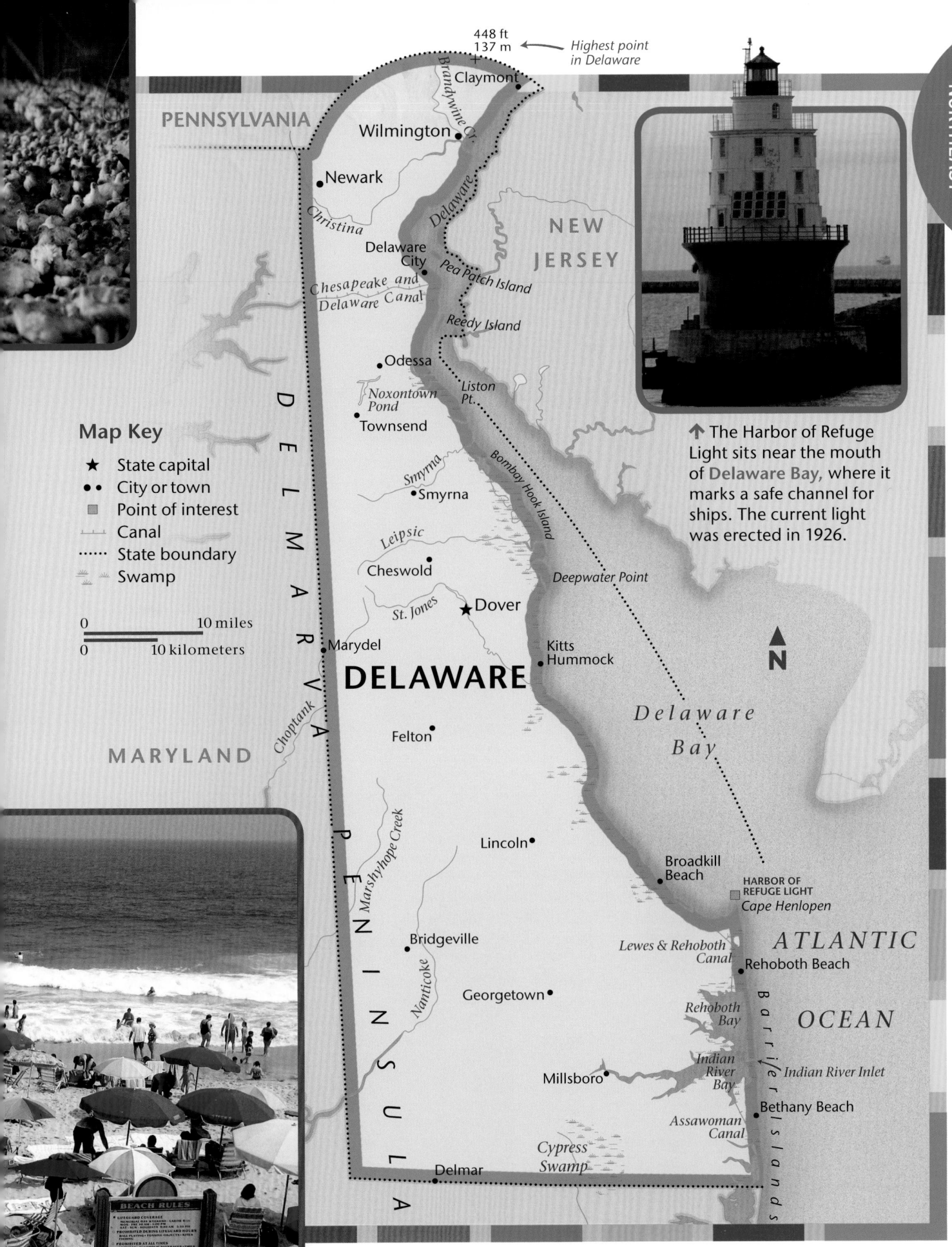

↑ The Harbor of Refuge Light sits near the mouth of **Delaware Bay,** where it marks a safe channel for ships. The current light was erected in 1926.

Maine

Land & Water The Appalachian Mountains, Mount Katahdin, and the Gulf of Maine are important land and water features of Maine.

Statehood Maine became the 23rd state in 1820.

People & Places Maine's population is 1,329,328. Augusta is the state capital. The largest city is Portland.

Fun Fact During the last ice age, glaciers carved hundreds of bays and inlets along Maine's shoreline and created some 2,000 islands off the coast.

↑ More than 60 lighthouses line Maine's rocky coastline, warning ships of danger. The oldest lighthouse, Portland Head Light, is located at **Cape Elizabeth.**

← Each year **Rockland** hosts the Maine Lobster Festival. This celebration of the state's popular seafood delicacy attracts visitors from far and near.

Maine State Flag

White Pine Cone and Tassel
State Flower

Chickadee
State Bird

↓ Moose are North America's largest deer, averaging six feet (2 m) tall at the shoulders. This female stands knee-deep in grass near **Rangeley Lake.**

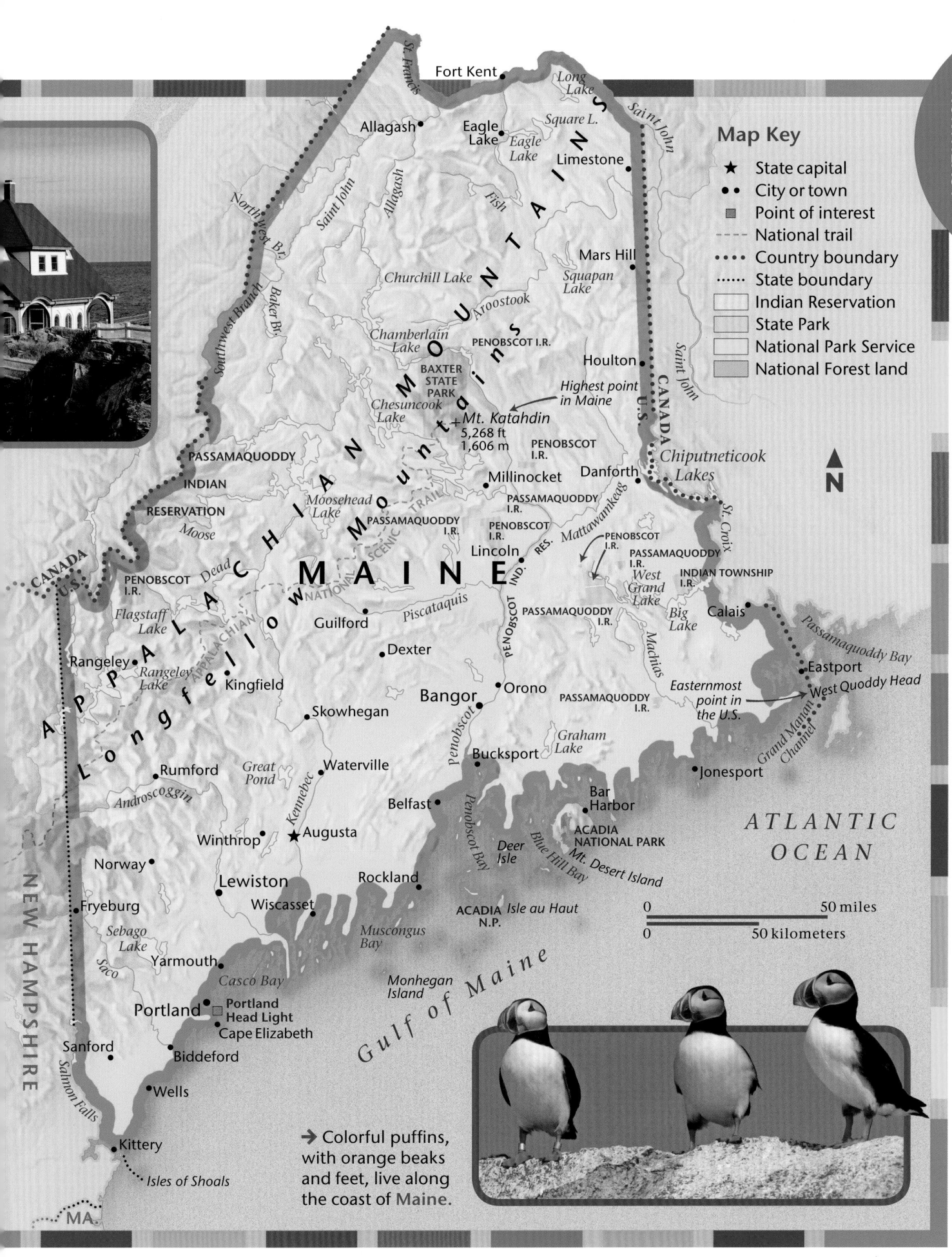

→ Colorful puffins, with orange beaks and feet, live along the coast of **Maine**.

Maryland

Land & Water The Appalachian Mountains, Potomac River, and Chesapeake Bay are important land and water features of Maryland.

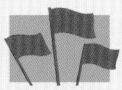

Statehood Maryland became the 7th state in 1788.

People & Places Maryland's population is 6,006,401. Annapolis is the state capital. The largest city is Baltimore.

Fun Fact The name of Baltimore's professional football team—the Ravens—may have been inspired by a poem written by the famous American author Edgar Allan Poe, who lived in Baltimore in the mid-1800s.

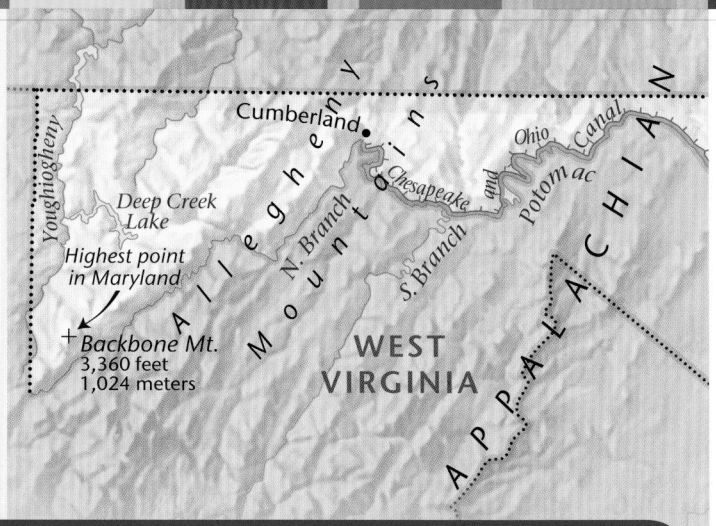

↑ Sailing is a popular pastime on Maryland's Chesapeake Bay. In the background, the **Bay Bridge** stretches 4.3 miles (6.9 km) across the waters of the bay.

Maryland State Flag

↑ Since the early 1700s, **Baltimore,** near the upper Chesapeake Bay, has been a major seaport and a focus of trade, industry, and immigration.

Black-Eyed Susan
State Flower

Northern (Baltimore) Oriole
State Bird

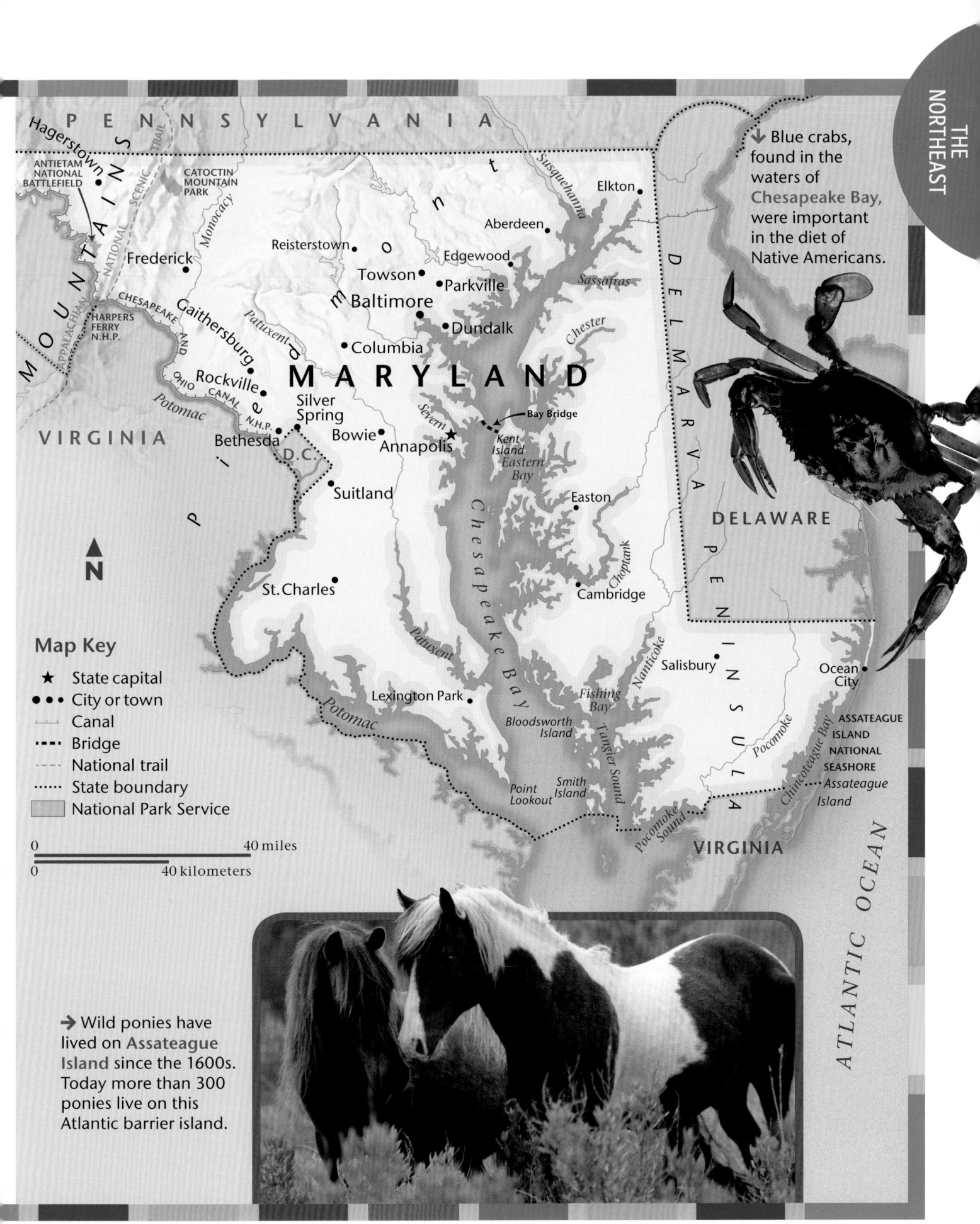

Blue crabs, found in the waters of **Chesapeake Bay,** were important in the diet of Native Americans.

Wild ponies have lived on **Assateague Island** since the 1600s. Today more than 300 ponies live on this Atlantic barrier island.

Massachusetts

Land & Water The Berkshires, Cape Cod, and Nantucket Sound are important land and water features of Massachusetts.

Statehood Massachusetts became the 6th state in 1788.

People & Places Massachusetts's population is 6,794,422. Boston is the state capital and the largest city.

Fun Fact In 1891 James Naismith invented the game of basketball as a form of physical activity. Today the Basketball Hall of Fame is located in Springfield in his honor.

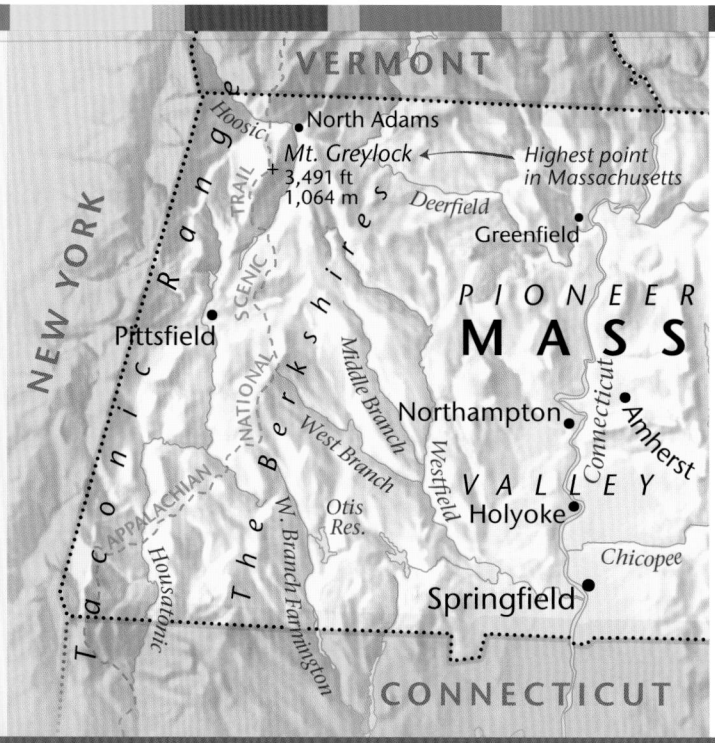

↑ Fenway Park in **Boston** is home to the Red Sox major league baseball team. The park was named for a Boston neighborhood known as the Fens.

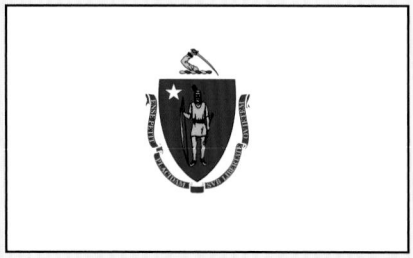

Massachusetts State Flag

Chickadee
State Bird

Mayflower
State Flower

↓ Cranberries are a major agricultural crop in Massachusetts, which produces 25 percent of the cranberries grown in the United States. An annual cranberry harvest festival is held in **Wareham**.

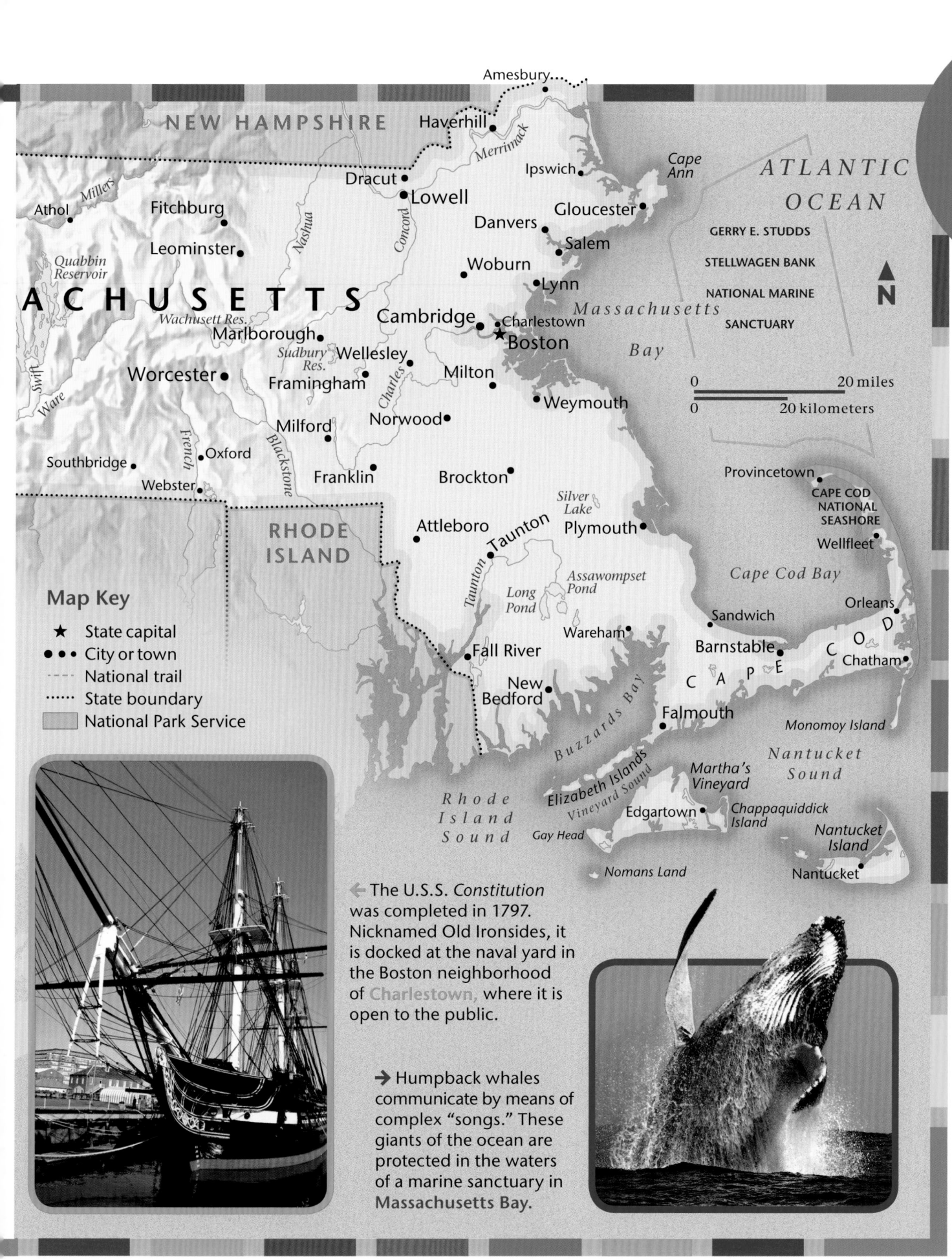

The U.S.S. *Constitution* was completed in 1797. Nicknamed Old Ironsides, it is docked at the naval yard in the Boston neighborhood of **Charlestown,** where it is open to the public.

Humpback whales communicate by means of complex "songs." These giants of the ocean are protected in the waters of a marine sanctuary in **Massachusetts Bay.**

New Hampshire

Land & Water The White Mountains, Mount Washington, and the Merrimack River are important land and water features of New Hampshire.

Statehood New Hampshire became the 9th state in 1788.

People & Places New Hampshire's population is 1,330,608. Concord is the state capital. The largest city is Manchester.

Fun Fact The first potato grown in the United States was planted in 1719 in Londonderry on the Common Field, now known simply as the Commons.

↑ A golden dome topped by a war eagle rises above New Hampshire's State House in **Concord**. The pale granite building was completed in 1819.

← Bitter cold and heavy snow are common in the **White Mountains** of New Hampshire, where snow tubing and skiing are popular winter sports.

New Hampshire State Flag

Purple Lilac
State Flower

Purple Finch
State Bird

↓ **Mount Washington** rises above trees rich with autumn colors. But soon winter will arrive, bringing some of the most extreme weather in the world.

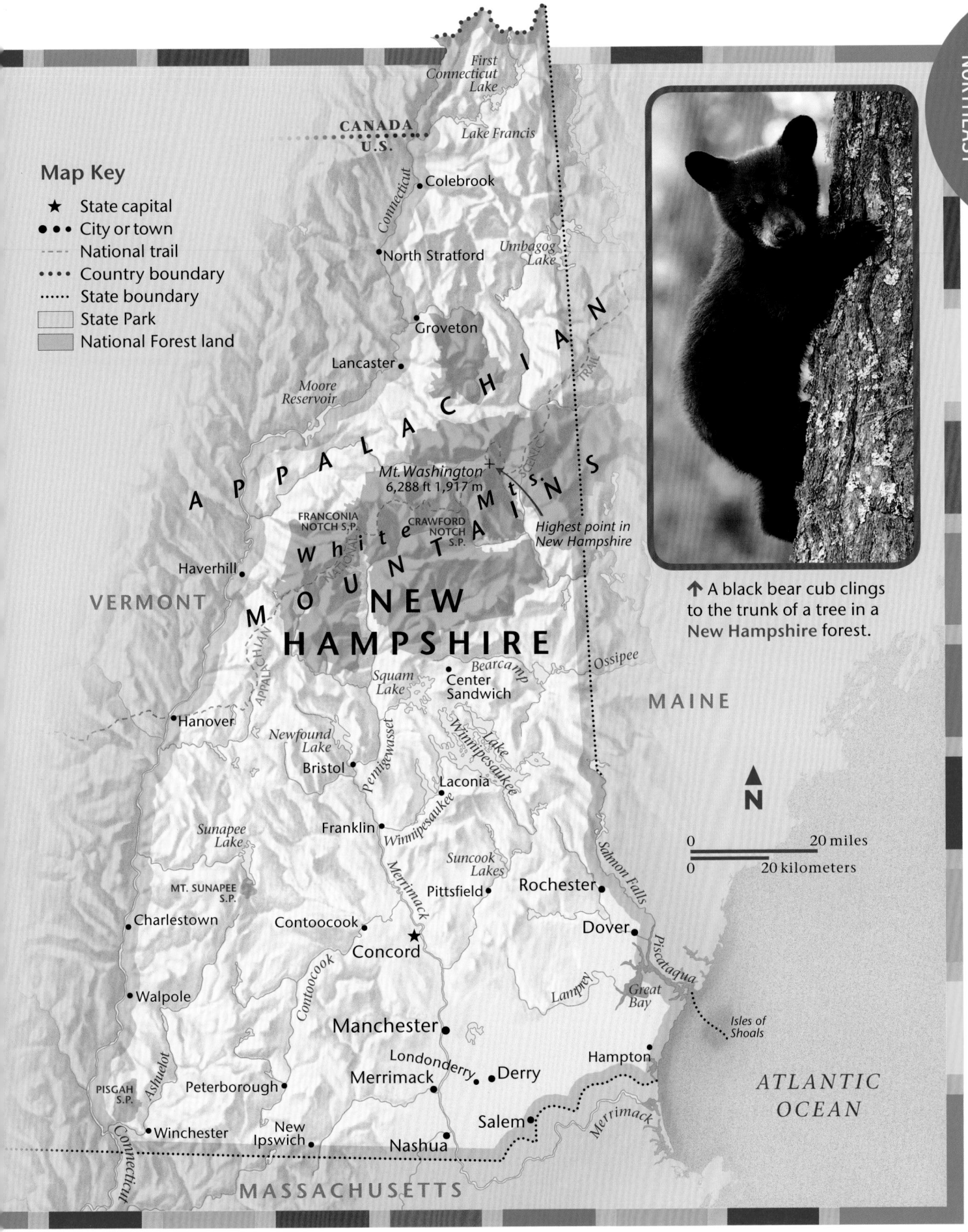

↑ A black bear cub clings to the trunk of a tree in a **New Hampshire** forest.

New Jersey

Land & Water The Kittatinny Mountains, Cape May, and the Delaware River are important land and water features of New Jersey.

Statehood New Jersey became the 3rd state in 1787.

People & Places New Jersey's population is 8,958,013. Trenton is the state capital. The largest city is Newark.

Fun Fact The first dinosaur skeleton found in North America was excavated at Haddonfield in 1858. It was named *Hadrosaurus* in honor of its discovery site.

↑ Sandy beaches on the Atlantic coast of New Jersey attract vacationers from near and far. Roller coasters are just one of the exciting rides in amusement parks along the shore.

← Street names, such as Boardwalk and Park Place, in the popular board game Monopoly are taken from actual street names in Atlantic City.

New Jersey State Flag

↓ The skylines of Jersey City (foreground) and New York City (in the distance at right) glow in the evening light. Jersey City, the second largest city in the state, is home to many large corporations.

American Goldfinch
State Bird

Violet
State Flower

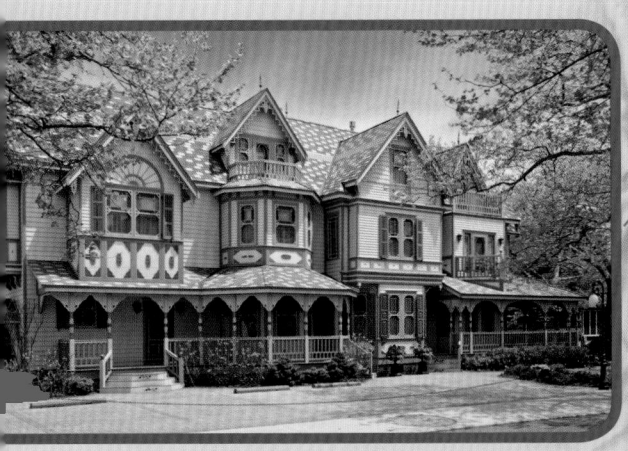

↑ Victorian-style houses line a street in **Cape May.** The town is a national historic landmark and the country's oldest seashore resort.

↑ New Jersey, known as the **Garden State,** is a leading producer of fresh fruits and vegetables.

NEW YORK
PENNSYLVANIA
NEW JERSEY
DELAWARE
ATLANTIC OCEAN
Delaware Bay
High Point 1,803 ft 550 m
Highest point in New Jersey
DELAWARE WATER GAP N.R.A.
APPALACHIAN NATIONAL SCENIC TRAIL
Kittatinny Mountains
Delaware
Wanaque Reservoir
Ringwood
Hudson
Sparta
Lake Hopatcong
Ridgewood
Paterson
Hackensack
Passaic
Muscoetcong
MORRISTOWN N.H.P.
Newark
New York
Jersey City
Ellis Island
Phillipsburg
Elizabeth
LOWER DELAWARE SCENIC & RECREATIONAL RIVER
Round Valley Res.
Woodbridge
GATEWAY N.R.A.
Lower Bay
Raritan
Edison
New Brunswick
Sandy Hook
Sandy Hook Bay
GATEWAY N.R.A.
East Brunswick
Delaware & Raritan Canal
Red Bank
Long Branch
Manalapan
Mercerville
Trenton
Asbury Park
Point Pleasant
Lakewood
Willingboro
Toms
Camden
Pennsauken
Toms River
Seaside Heights
Cherry Hill
Haddonfield
Barnegat Bay
Mullica
PINELANDS NATIONAL RESERVE
Glassboro
Salem
Pennsville
Long Beach Island
Hammonton
Ship Bottom
Maurice
Little Egg Harbor
Beach Haven
GREAT EGG HARBOR NATIONAL SCENIC AND RECREATIONAL RIVER
Great Egg Harbor
Great Bay
Vineland
Bridgeton
Cohansey
Millville
Atlantic City
Ventnor City
Somers Point
Tuckahoe
Ocean City
Cape May Court House
CAPE MAY
Cape May
N
0 20 miles
0 20 kilometers

Map Key

- ★ State capital
- City or town
- Canal
- National trail
- State boundary
- Swamp
- National Park Service

New York

Land & Water The Adirondack Mountains, the Finger Lakes, and the Hudson River are important land and water features of New York.

Statehood New York became the 11th state in 1788.

People & Places New York's population is 19,795,791. Albany is the state capital. The largest city is New York City.

Fun Fact The Erie Canal, built in the 1820s, connected Buffalo to the Hudson River at Albany, allowing ships to travel from the Atlantic Ocean to the Great Lakes. The canal contributed to the growth of New York City as a major trade center.

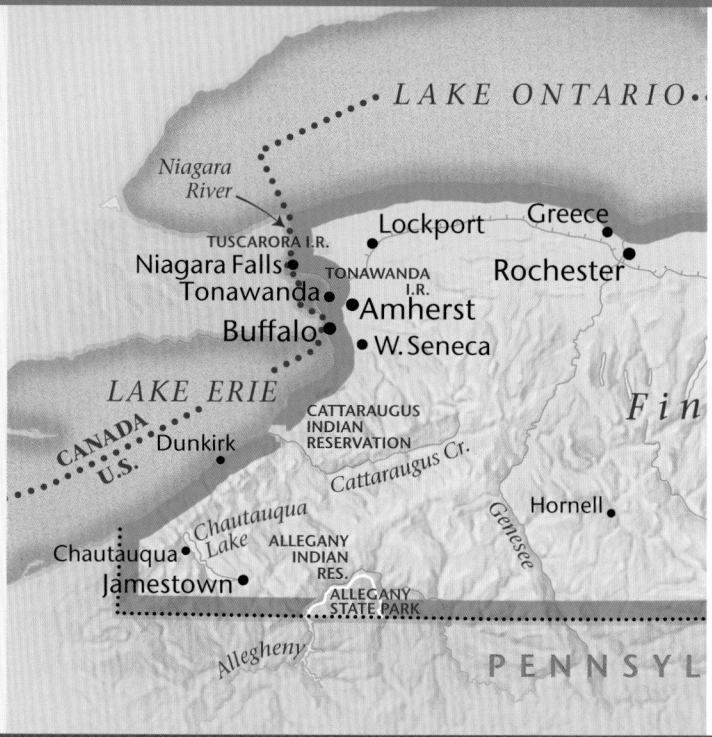

New York State Flag

Eastern Bluebird
State Bird

Rose
State Flower

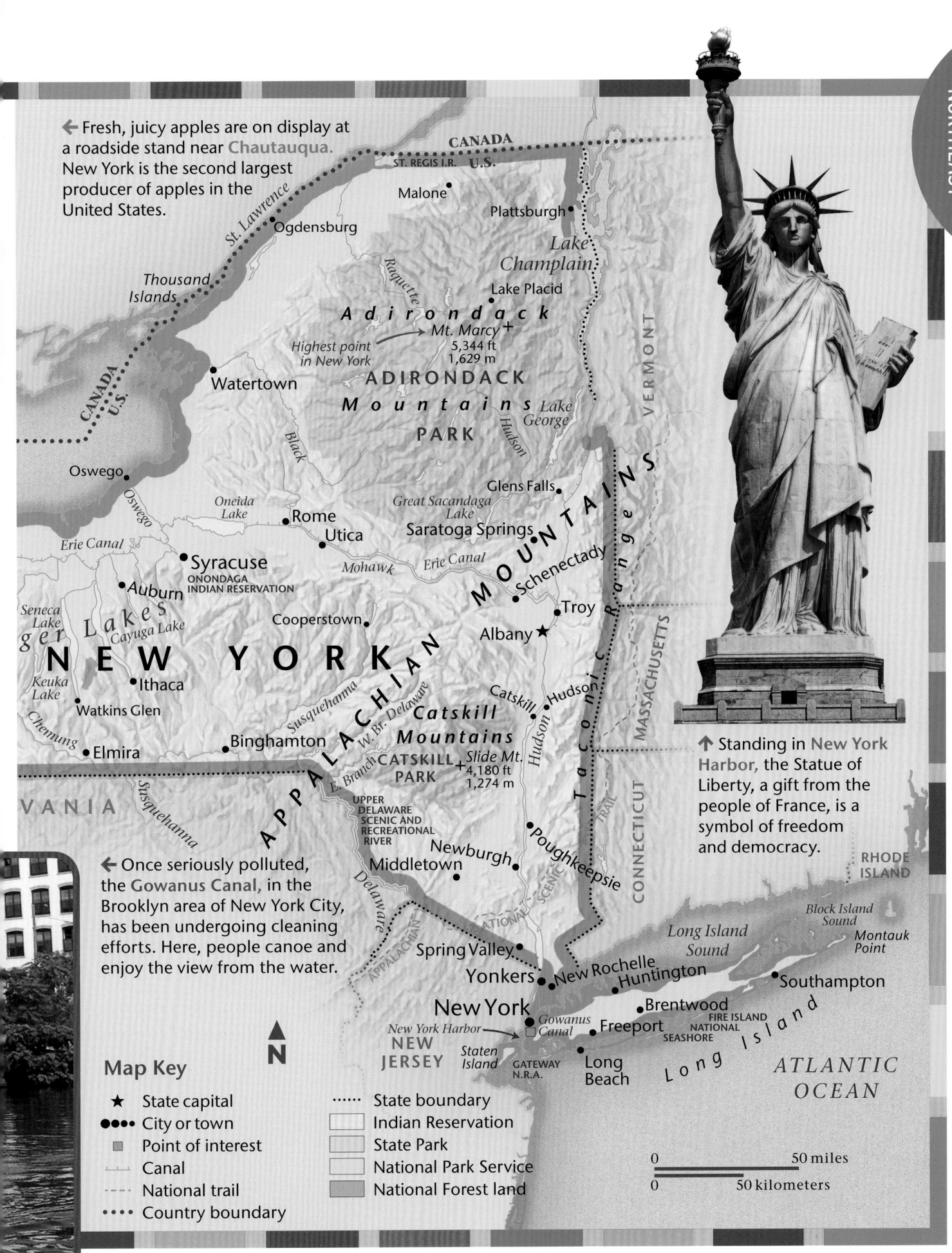

← Fresh, juicy apples are on display at a roadside stand near **Chautauqua.** New York is the second largest producer of apples in the United States.

↑ Standing in **New York Harbor,** the Statue of Liberty, a gift from the people of France, is a symbol of freedom and democracy.

← Once seriously polluted, the **Gowanus Canal,** in the Brooklyn area of New York City, has been undergoing cleaning efforts. Here, people canoe and enjoy the view from the water.

Map Key

- ★ State capital
- City or town
- Point of interest
- Canal
- National trail
- Country boundary
- State boundary
- Indian Reservation
- State Park
- National Park Service
- National Forest land

PENNSYLVANIA

Pennsylvania

Land & Water The Allegheny Mountains, the Pocono Mountains, and the Susquehanna River are important land and water features of Pennsylvania.

Statehood Pennsylvania became the 2nd state in 1787.

People & Places Pennsylvania's population is 12,802,503. Harrisburg is the state capital. The largest city is Philadelphia.

Fun Fact The town of Hershey is known as the Chocolate Capital of the World. The Hershey Company exports its chocolate candies to some 70 countries around the world.

LAKE ERIE
Erie
Corry
Allegheny Reservoir
Meadville
Titusville
Pymatuning Reservoir
Allegheny
Greenville
OHIO
Clarion
Sharon
Clarion
Beaver
Punxsutawney
New Castle
PENN
Kittanning
Allegheny
Indiana
Ohio
McCandless
Conemaugh
Pittsburgh
Penn Hills
Johnstown
Washington
Highest point in Pennsylvania
Mt. Davis 3,213 ft 979 m
Morrisville
Uniontown
Monongahela
Youghiogheny
Cheat
WEST VIRGINIA
Allegheny

Map Key

- ★ State capital
- ●●●● City or town
- ---- National trail
- ····· State boundary
- National Park Service
- National Forest land

Pennsylvania State Flag

Mountain Laurel
State Flower

Ruffed Grouse
State Bird

← The **Appalachian Trail** stretches across more than 2,000 miles (3,200 km) from Maine to Georgia. The trail passes through 14 states, including Pennsylvania.

NEW YORK
Chemung
Susquehanna
Bradford
Sayre
Allegheny
Coudersport
Mansfield
Tioga
Wellsboro
Pine Creek
Pine Creek Gorge
Towanda
UPPER DELAWARE SCENIC AND RECREATIONAL RIVER
Delaware
Carbondale
St. Marys
Scranton
Lake Wallenpaupack
West Branch Susquehanna
Williamsport
Wilkes-Barre
Pocono Mts.
DELAWARE WATER GAP NATIONAL RECREATION AREA
Lock Haven
Bloomsburg
Susquehanna
Clearfield
Stroudsburg
Sunbury
State College
Lehigh
Pottsville
Bethlehem
Easton
Allentown
NEW JERSEY
Altoona
Juniata
Raystown Lake
Tuscarora Mountain
NATIONAL
SCENIC
TRAIL
Schuylkill
Reading
Doylestown
Delaware
Hershey
Harrisburg
Carlisle
Three Mile Island
Elizabethtown
Norristown
Levittown
VALLEY FORGE N.H.P.
Bedford
Lancaster
Upper Darby
Philadelphia
Chambersburg
York
Chester
Gettysburg
GETTYSBURG N.H.P.
Waynesboro
MARYLAND
W.VA.
DELAWARE
0 40 miles
0 40 kilometers
N

← **Pittsburgh** was established in 1758 where the Monongahela and Allegheny Rivers meet to form the Ohio River. Today it is a center of finance, medicine, education, and robotics.

→ The Liberty Bell, cast in 1753 by Pennsylvania craftsmen, hangs in **Philadelphia.** Because of a crack, it is no longer rung.

Rhode Island

Land & Water Block Island and Narragansett Bay, with its many islands, are important land and water features of Rhode Island.

Statehood Rhode Island became the 13th state in 1790.

People & Places Rhode Island's population is 1,056,298. Providence is the state capital and the largest city.

Fun Fact Rhode Island is the smallest U.S. state in size. It measures just 48 miles (77 km) from north to south and 37 miles (60 km) from east to west.

↑ Sailing is a popular sport in Rhode Island. This boat is in full sail on a late summer day on **Narragansett Bay.**

← The North Lighthouse on the northern tip of **Block Island** still warns ships of dangerous waters. The building, constructed in 1867, does not have a typical lighthouse design.

Rhode Island State Flag

Violet
State Flower

Rhode Island Red
State Bird

↓ Rhode Island has cold, snowy winters. Skaters enjoy ice-skating on City Center public rink in front of the historic city hall in **Providence.**

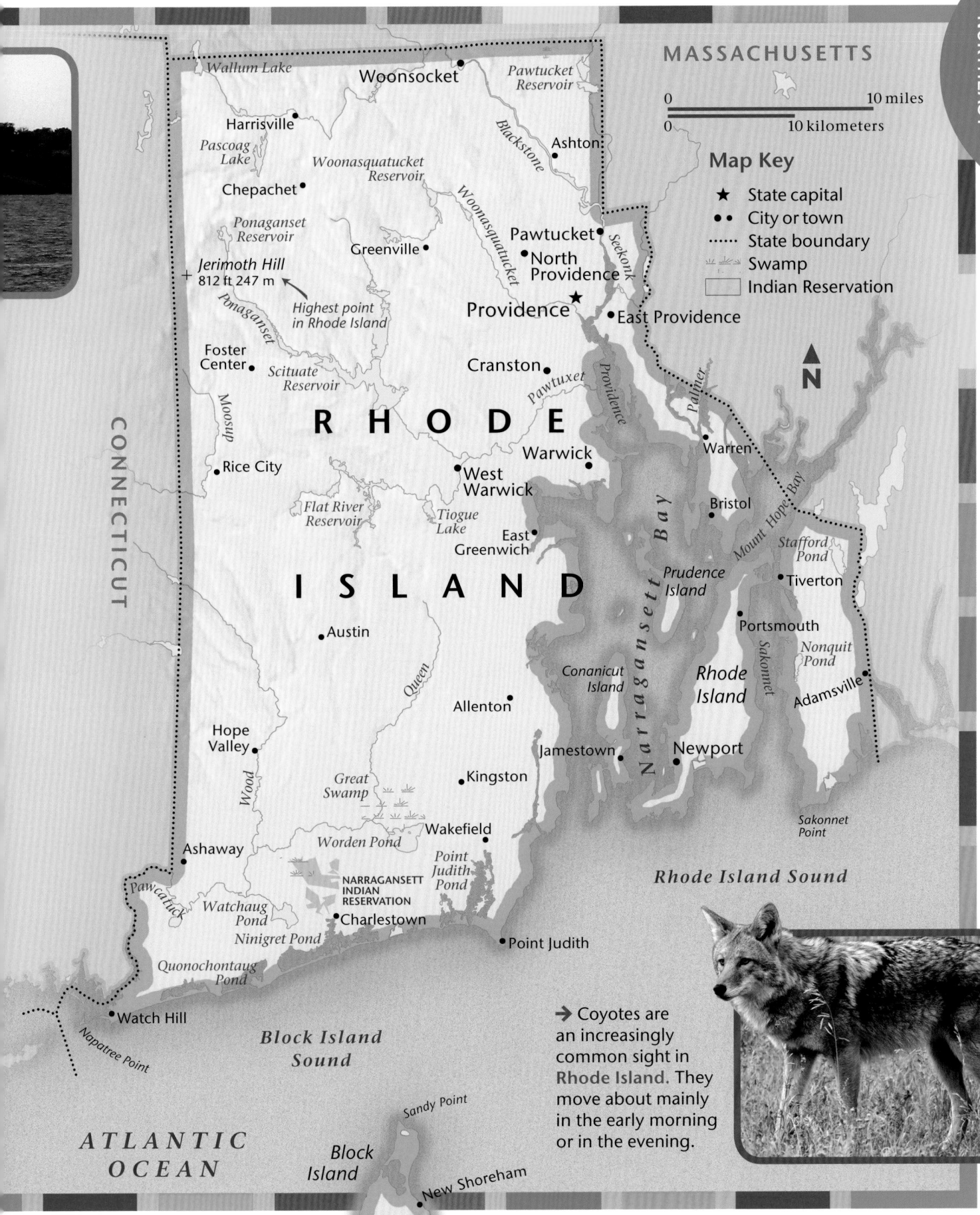

→ Coyotes are an increasingly common sight in **Rhode Island.** They move about mainly in the early morning or in the evening.

Vermont

Land & Water The Green Mountains, Lake Champlain, and the Connecticut River are important land and water features of Vermont.

Statehood Vermont became the 14th state in 1791.

People & Places Vermont's population is 626,042. Montpelier is the state capital. The largest city is Burlington.

Fun Fact From the end of the Revolutionary War until 1791, Vermont was an independent republic with its own government and money. It even thought about uniting with Canada.

Vermont State Flag

Red Clover
State Flower

Hermit Thrush
State Bird

↑ Vermont ice cream is famous worldwide. The headquarters of Ben & Jerry's in **Burlington** is the number one tourist attraction in the state.

↑ People collect the sap of maple trees, which is boiled to make maple sugar and syrup. Maple production is celebrated each year at a festival in **Tunbridge**.

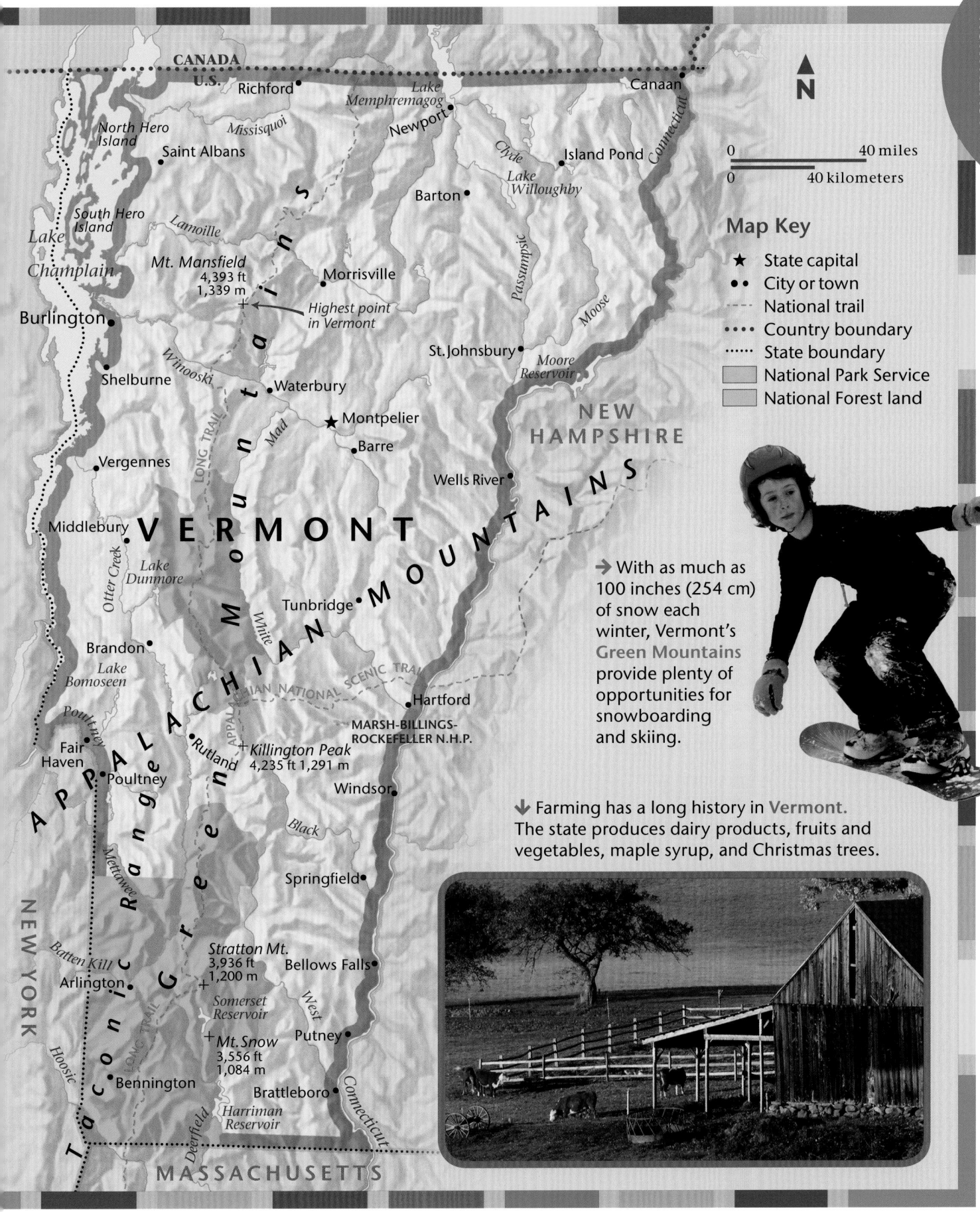

→ With as much as 100 inches (254 cm) of snow each winter, Vermont's **Green Mountains** provide plenty of opportunities for snowboarding and skiing.

↓ Farming has a long history in **Vermont.** The state produces dairy products, fruits and vegetables, maple syrup, and Christmas trees.

The Southeast

The Southeast region of the United States is full of variety, both in its landscape and in its history. The Appalachian Mountains are old and worn down. The coastal margins are marked by barrier islands and wetlands. And in the western part of the region, the Mississippi River flows out through a broad delta into the Gulf of Mexico. The region, with roots in agriculture, suffered great destruction during the Civil War, but today it is a part of the Sunbelt, where cities are growing rapidly and the economy is shifting to high-tech industries.

Live oak trees, some hundreds of years old, form a natural arch across a country road in Georgia. These trees, draped in Spanish moss, are common in the coastal Southeast. Flamingos are a familiar sight in parks in Florida.

Alabama

Land & Water The Appalachian Mountains, the Cumberland Plateau, and Mobile Bay are important land and water features of Alabama.

Statehood Alabama became the 22nd state in 1819.

People & Places Alabama's population is 4,858,979. Montgomery is the state capital. The largest city is Birmingham.

Fun Fact In Magnolia Springs, on Mobile Bay, mail is delivered by boat. This city has the country's only year-round, all-water mail route used by the U.S. Postal Service.

↑ Southern Alabama has a narrow coastline fronting the Gulf of Mexico. The beach resort of **Gulf Shores** is a popular tourist destination.

↑ A welder repairs a boat in **Bayou La Batre** on Alabama's Gulf coast. The town is a center for shipbuilding and seafood processing.

Alabama State Flag

Northern Flicker
State Bird

Camellia
State Flower

↓ This old railroad bridge, built in 1839, was a toll bridge across the **Tennessee River.** Today it is a pedestrian bridge.

The bobwhite quail is common throughout Alabama. It builds its nest on the ground and lives on a diet of seeds.

Arkansas

Land & Water The Ouachita Mountains, the Ozark Plateau, and the Mississippi River are important land and water features of Arkansas.

Statehood Arkansas became the 25th state in 1836.

People & Places Arkansas has a population of 2,978,204. Little Rock is the state capital and the largest city.

Fun Fact In 1924 Crater of Diamonds State Park near Murfreesboro yielded the largest natural diamond ever found in the United States. The stone, called "Uncle Sam," weighed more than 40 carats.

↑ Located in the River Market District of Little Rock, the Museum of Discovery offers children interactive experiences in science, technology, engineering, and math.

Arkansas State Flag

Apple Blossom
State Flower

Mockingbird
State Bird

↑ A farmer in eastern Arkansas checks the progress of his rice crop. The state is a leading producer of rice.

MISSOURI
OZARK PLATEAU
OKLAHOMA
TENNESSEE
MISSISSIPPI
TEXAS
LOUISIANA
ARKANSAS
Rogers
Berryville
Beaver Lake
Springdale
Bull Shoals Lake
Mountain Home
Norfork Lake
Pocahontas
Buffalo
BUFFALO NATIONAL RIVER
White
Black
Mississippi
Jonesboro
Mountain View
Batesville
Boston Mountains
Trumann
Clinton
Newport
Marked Tree
Van Buren
Ozark
Lake Dardanelle
Arkansas
Greers Ferry Lake
Heber Springs
St. Francis
Fort Smith
Russellville
Searcy
Wynne
West Memphis
Highest point in Arkansas
Magazine Mt.
2,753 ft
839 m
Conway
Cache
Waldron
Brinkley
Jacksonville
North Little Rock
Little Rock
Ouachita Mountains
Lake Ouachita
Mena
HOT SPRINGS N.P.
Hot Springs
Benton
West Helena
Helena
Stuttgart
Malvern
De Gray Lake
Pine Bluff
Arkansas
Murfreesboro
Arkadelphia
Saline
Bayou Bartholomew
DeQueen
Crater of Diamonds S.P.
Little Missouri
Dumas
Millwood Lake
Fordyce
Ashdown
Hope
Red
Warren
Camden
Ouachita
Dermott
Texarkana
Stamps
Magnolia
El Dorado
Lake Jack Lee
Crossett
N
Map Key
★ State capital
City or town
Point of interest
State boundary
National Park Service
National Forest land
0 50 miles
0 50 kilometers

← The White River flows through the Ozark Plateau. Its cold water is a perfect habitat for trout, a popular sport fish.

Florida

Land & Water The Florida Keys, the Everglades, and Lake Okeechobee are important land and water features of Florida.

Statehood Florida became the 27th state in 1845.

People & Places Florida's population is 20,271,272. Tallahassee is the state capital. The largest city is Jacksonville.

Fun Fact Everglades National Park is home to rare and endangered species such as the American crocodile, the Florida panther, and the West Indian manatee.

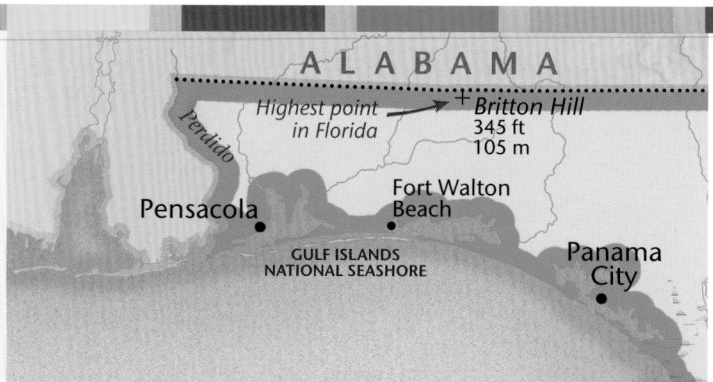

The manatee is the state marine mammal of **Florida**. It averages ten feet (3 m) in length and can weigh 1,000 pounds (450 kg).

NASA's new Space Launch System, the most powerful rocket in history, will lift off from **Kennedy Space Center** in 2018.

Florida State Flag

Orange Blossom
State Flower

Mockingbird
State Bird

↑ Two young boys get ready to explore the warm waters near John Pennekamp Coral Reef State Park in the **Florida Keys.**

↓ **Orange County,** in central Florida, is a major producer of citrus fruit. Florida is the leading orange producer in the United States.

Georgia

Land & Water The Sea Islands, the Okefenokee Swamp, and the Savannah River are important land and water features of Georgia.

Statehood Georgia became the 4th state in 1788.

People & Places Georgia's population is 10,214,860. Atlanta is the state capital and the largest city.

Fun Fact The Georgia Aquarium in Atlanta is the largest aquarium in the world. It features more than 100,000 animals living in more than eight million gallons (30.3 million L) of water.

← Built for the 1996 Olympic Games, Centennial Olympic Park in **Atlanta** is the site of festivals and community events that attract an estimated three million visitors each year.

→ Nearly half the peanut crop in the United States is grown in Georgia. **Sylvester** is the peanut capital of the world.

Georgia State Flag

Cherokee Rose
State Flower

Brown Thrasher
State Bird

↓ Alligators, which can live more than 50 years, are found in marshes, rivers, and swamps, including those in the **Okefenokee National Wildlife Refuge.**

THE SOUTHEAST

↓ Peaches, a leading state crop, were introduced to Georgia's **Sea Islands** in 1571.

Kentucky

Land & Water Mammoth Cave, Lake Cumberland, and the Ohio River are important land and water features of Kentucky.

Statehood Kentucky became the 15th state in 1792.

People & Places Kentucky's population is 4,425,092. Frankfort is the state capital. The largest city is Louisville.

Fun Fact The song "Happy Birthday to You," one of the most popular songs in the English language, was written in 1893 by two sisters living in Louisville.

→ Shaker Village in **Pleasant Hill** preserves the culture and history of this important social movement.

← Abraham Lincoln, the 16th U.S. president, was born near **Hodgenville.** His profile appears on the penny.

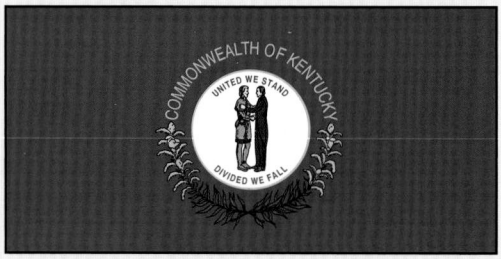

Kentucky State Flag

Goldenrod
State Flower

Cardinal
State Bird

↓ The setting sun turns the sky red over **Cave Run Lake.** The lake is a popular vacation spot because of its natural beauty.

Map Key
★ State capital
●●● City or town
····· State boundary
Pass
National Park Service
National Forest land

N

0 50 miles
0 50 kilometers

OHIO
INDIANA
WEST VIRGINIA
VIRGINIA
TENNESSEE
KENTUCKY
BLUE GRASS REGION
Covington
Florence
Williamstown
Maysville
Vanceburg
Ashland
La Grange
Flemingsburg
Frankfort
Paris
Louisville
Jeffersontown
Georgetown
Lexington
Winchester
Radcliff
Pleasant Hill
Richmond
Owensboro
Elizabethtown
Hodgenville
Prestonsburg
Jackson
Pikeville
Leitchfield
Campbellsville
Mount Vernon
Somerset
London
Cumberland
Highest point in Kentucky
Black Mt. 4,145 ft 1,263 m
Cumberland Mts.
Cumberland Gap
CUMBERLAND GAP N.H.P.
Middlesboro
MAMMOTH CAVE NATIONAL PARK
Cave City
Bowling Green
Glasgow
Franklin
Albany
BIG SOUTH FORK NAT. RIVER & REC. AREA
Ohio
Licking
Kentucky
Salt
Red
Rockcastle
Big Sandy
Tug Fork
Cave Run Lake
Rough River Lake
Nolin River Lake
Green
Green River Lake
Barren River Lake
Cumberland
Lake Cumberland
Dale Hollow Lake
Cumberland Plateau
Pine Mountain
APPALACHIAN MOUNTAINS

← Riders in colorful jerseys astride powerful race horses charge out of the starting gate during a race in **Kentucky.** The state is a major producer of Thoroughbred race horses.

Louisiana

Land & Water Driskill Mountain, Lake Pontchartrain, and the Mississippi River are important land and water features of Louisiana.

Statehood Louisiana became the 18th state in 1812.

People & Places Louisiana's population is 4,670,724. Baton Rouge is the state capital. The largest city is New Orleans.

Fun Fact The Louisiana state capitol building in Baton Rouge is the tallest of all the state capitols. It is a limestone skyscraper that stands 450 feet (137 m) tall and has 34 stories!

↑ Musicians practice on a park bench in **New Orleans** as they wait for one of the city's Mardi Gras parades to begin.

↑ The *Mississippi Queen*, a paddle-wheel boat, churns up the water as it steams along the Mississippi River between **Baton Rouge** and New Orleans.

Louisiana State Flag

Magnolia
State Flower

Brown Pelican
State Bird

← Louisiana is a leading producer of shrimp in the United States. Most of it is harvested from the **Barataria-Terrebonne** estuary of the Mississippi River.

Springhill
Red
Caddo Lake
Caddo Black Bayou Preserve
Bossier City
Shreveport
Lake Bistineau
Mansfield
Red
Toledo Bend Reservoir
Natchitoches
Many
Leesville
De Ridder
Sabine
Lake Charles
TEXAS
Sabine Lake
Calcasieu Lake

→ A colorful mask decorated with ribbons is a reminder of Mardi Gras, which is celebrated in **Louisiana** in late winter each year.

↑ The **Caddo Black Bayou Preserve** (near Caddo Lake), a natural wetland with hardwood forest, cypress swamps, and rare plant species, is a protected area that is closed to the public.

Mississippi

Land & Water The Mississippi Petrified Forest, the Tennessee-Tombigbee Waterway, and the Mississippi River are important land and water features of Mississippi.

Statehood Mississippi became the 20th state in 1817.

People & Places Mississippi's population is 2,992,333. Jackson is the state capital and the largest city.

Fun Fact Jim Henson, creator of Kermit the Frog, Miss Piggy, Big Bird, and other famous Muppets, was born in Greenville.

↑ Mississippi is the leading producer of catfish in the United States. A part of the **Mississippi River Valley** known as the Delta is the main producing area.

↑ Two bridges stretch across the Mississippi River in the city of **Vicksburg.** The river is home to more than 400 species of wildlife.

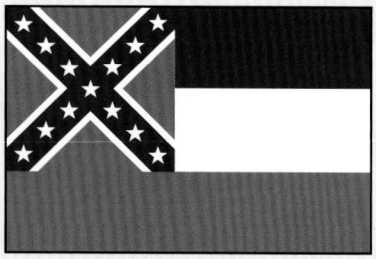

Mississippi State Flag

Mockingbird
State Bird

Magnolia
State Flower

↓ Children play in a tidal pool on a **Biloxi** beach as the sun sets. Barrier islands separate the city from the Gulf of Mexico.

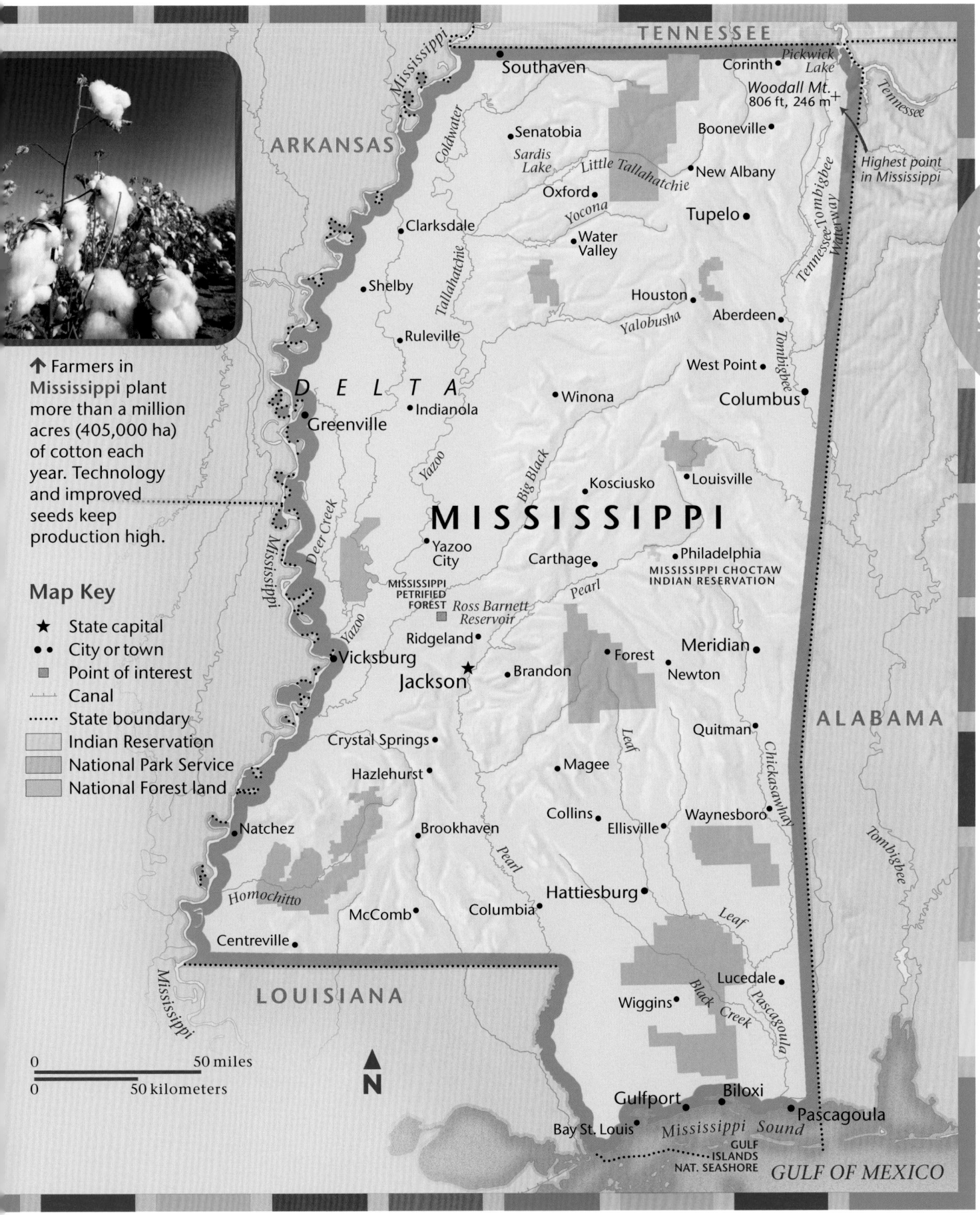

↑ Farmers in **Mississippi** plant more than a million acres (405,000 ha) of cotton each year. Technology and improved seeds keep production high.

Map Key

- ★ State capital
- •• City or town
- ■ Point of interest
- Canal
- ····· State boundary
- Indian Reservation
- National Park Service
- National Forest land

North Carolina

Land & Water Mount Mitchell, Lake Norman, and the Cape Fear River are important land and water features of North Carolina.

Statehood North Carolina became the 12th state in 1789.

People & Places North Carolina's population is 10,042,802. Raleigh is the state capital. The largest city is Charlotte.

Fun Fact The University of North Carolina, the first public university in the United States, opened its doors in 1795 with 2 professors and 41 students.

North Carolina State Flag

Cardinal
State Bird

Flowering Dogwood
State Flower

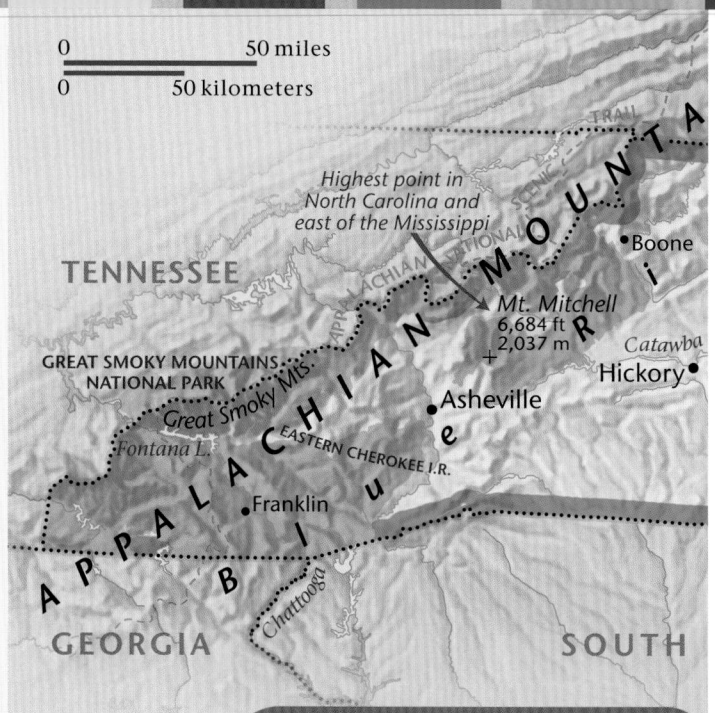

↑ The chapel tower is a landmark on the campus of Duke University in **Durham.**

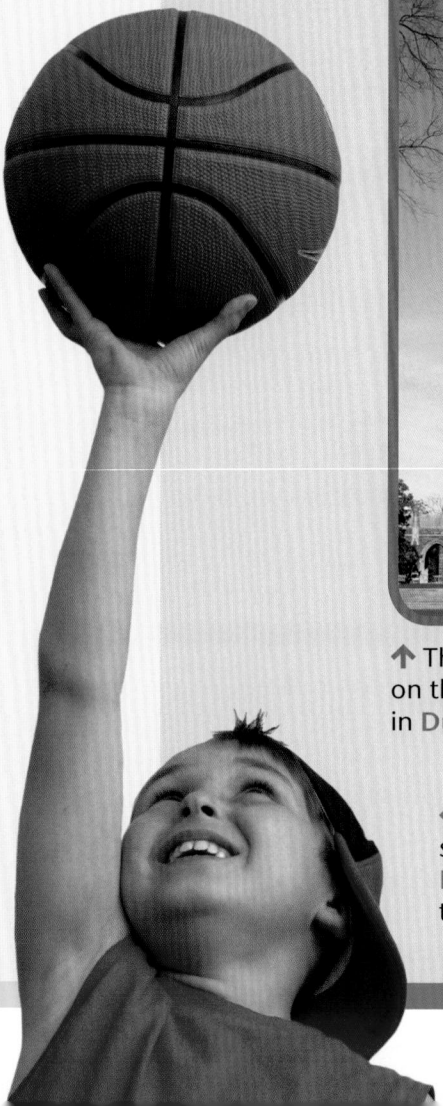

← Basketball is a popular sport among all ages in **North Carolina,** whether on the court or in the backyard.

VIRGINIA
NORTH CAROLINA
SOUTH CAROLINA
ATLANTIC OCEAN
Mt. Airy
John H. Kerr Reservoir
Lake Gaston
Roanoke Rapids
Great Dismal Swamp
Elizabeth City
Edenton
Kitty Hawk
Roanoke Island
Albemarle Sound
Yadkin
Greensboro
Winston-Salem
High Point
Burlington
Chapel Hill
Falls L.
Durham
Rocky Mount
Raleigh
B. Everett Jordan Lake
Cary
Wilson
Williamston
Greenville
Lake Norman
Salisbury
Kannapolis
Concord
Gastonia
Charlotte
Monroe
Pinehurst
Dunn
Goldsboro
Kinston
New Bern
Fayetteville
Jacksonville
Havelock
Morehead City
Cape Lookout Lighthouse
Cape Lookout
Onslow Bay
Lumberton
Whiteville
Lake Waccamaw
Green Swamp
Wilmington
Wrightsville Beach
Southport
Cape Fear
Long Bay
Hatteras Island
CAPE HATTERAS NATIONAL SEASHORE
Cape Hatteras
Ocracoke Island
Outer Banks
Pamlico Sounds
CAPE LOOKOUT NATIONAL SEASHORE
Roanoke
Chowan
Tar
Neuse
Pee Dee
Deep
Lumber
South
Cape Fear
N

Map Key

- ★ State capital
- ●●● City or town
- ■ Point of interest
- National trail
- State boundary
- Swamp
- Indian Reservation
- National Park Service
- National Forest land

← Cape Lookout Lighthouse on the **Outer Banks** has warned ships of dangerous sandbars since it began operation in 1812.

→ Orville and Wilbur Wright, from Dayton, Ohio, made the first successful airplane flight near **Kitty Hawk** on North Carolina's Outer Banks.

South Carolina

Land & Water Sumter National Forest, Lake Marion, and the Great Pee Dee River are important land and water features of South Carolina.

Statehood South Carolina became the 8th state in 1788.

People & Places South Carolina's population is 4,896,146. Columbia is the state capital and the largest city.

Fun Fact Sweetgrass baskets have been made in the coastal lowland region for more than 300 years. They were originally used in the planting and processing of rice.

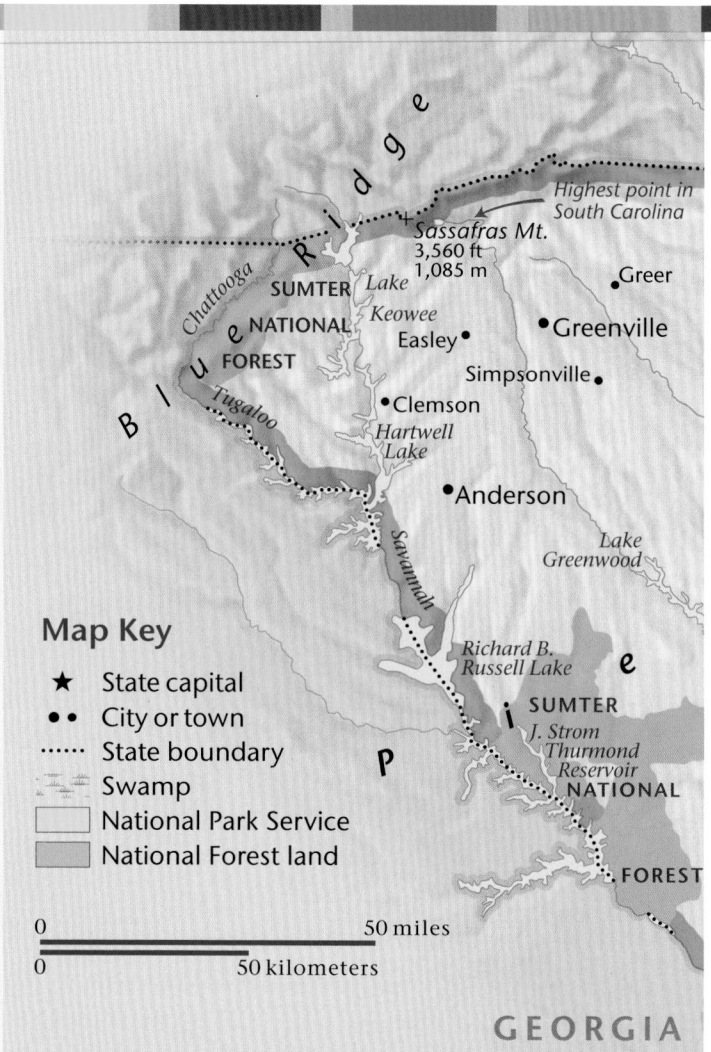

Large container ships carrying valuable manufactured goods link South Carolina to the global economy. **Charleston** is the state's largest port.

South Carolina State Flag

Yellow Jessamine
State Flower

Carolina Wren
State Bird

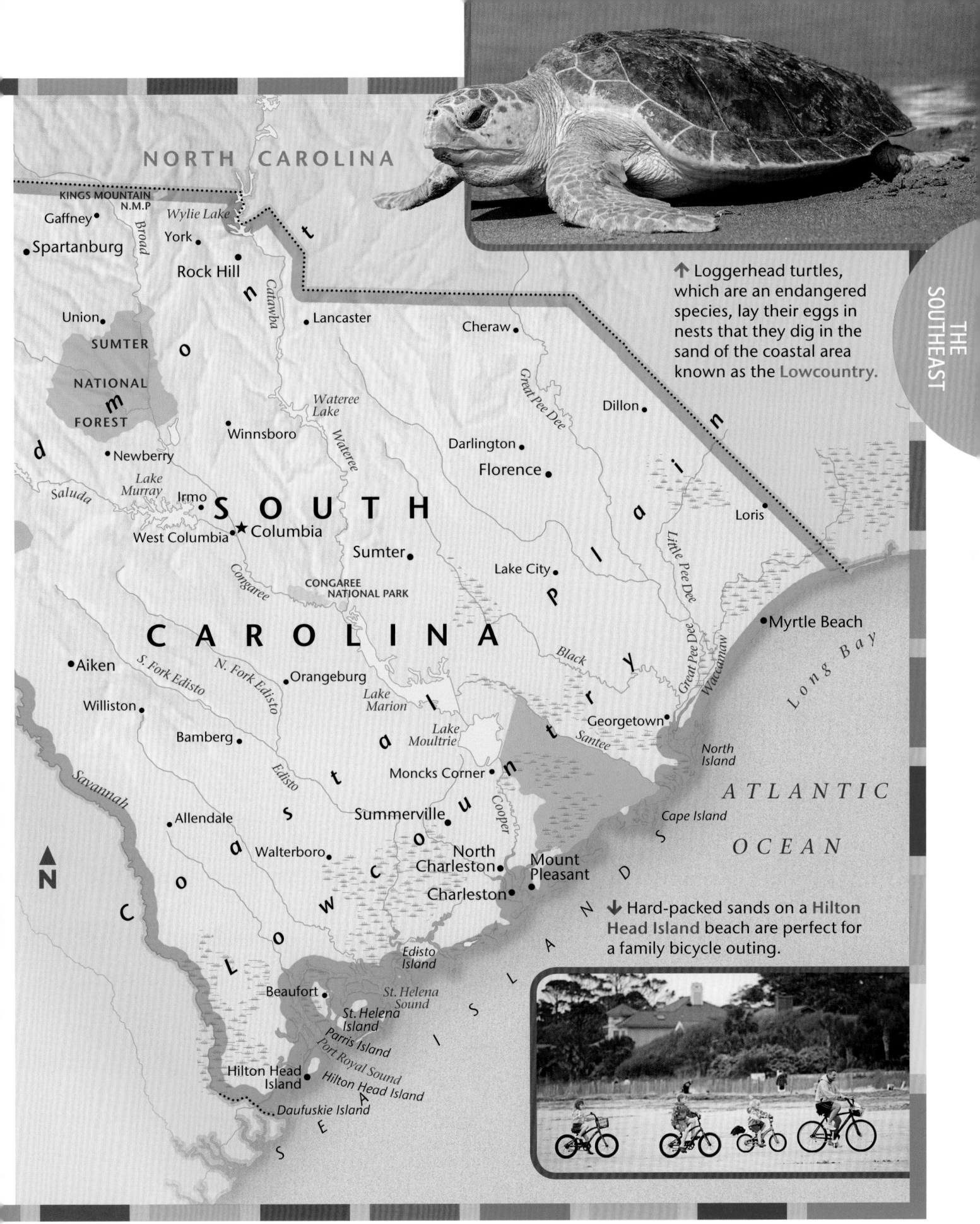

↑ Loggerhead turtles, which are an endangered species, lay their eggs in nests that they dig in the sand of the coastal area known as the **Lowcountry.**

↓ Hard-packed sands on a **Hilton Head Island** beach are perfect for a family bicycle outing.

Tennessee

Land & Water The Cumberland Plateau, Reelfoot Lake, and the Tennessee River are important land and water features of Tennessee.

Statehood Tennessee became the 16th state in 1796.

People & Places Tennessee's population is 6,600,299. Nashville is the state capital. The largest city is Memphis.

Fun Fact In 1811–1812 three major earthquakes, known as the New Madrid earthquakes, changed the landscape in parts of Tennessee and Missouri. The ground in northwest Tennessee sank, creating Reelfoot Lake.

→ **Memphis** is famous for its barbecue, especially baby back ribs that are cooked so long that the meat falls from the bones.

Tennessee State Flag

Iris
State Flower

Mockingbird
State Bird

↓ Norris Dam, on a tributary of the Tennessee River, was completed in 1936. It was constructed to generate electricity.

KENTUCKY
VIRGINIA
NORTH CAROLINA
SOUTH CAROLINA
GEORGIA
ALABAMA
TENNESSEE

0 50 miles
0 50 kilometers

Barkley
Springfield
Clarksville
Cumberland
Old Hickory L.
Nashville★
Hendersonville
Lebanon
Franklin
Smyrna
J. Percy Priest Lake
Duck
Murfreesboro
Columbia
Buffalo
Lewisburg
Shelbyville
Pulaski
Tims Ford Lake
Chattanooga
Tennessee
Dale Hollow Lake
BIG SOUTH FORK NATIONAL RIVER AND RECREATION AREA
Cookeville
Center Hill Lake
Sparta
Chickamauga Lake
Cumberland Plateau
Knoxville
Oak Ridge
Watts Bar Lake
Tellico Lake
Athens
Cleveland
Norris Lake
CUMBERLAND GAP N.H.P.
Clinch
Bristol
Kingsport
Johnson City
Cherokee Lake
Morristown
Douglas Lake
Sevierville
Newport
Fort Loudoun Lake
Gatlinburg
Maryville
Great Smoky Mts.
APPALACHIAN MOUNTAINS
Clingmans Dome
6,643 ft 2,025 m
GREAT SMOKY MOUNTAINS NATIONAL PARK
Highest point in Tennessee
Hiwassee
French Broad
Nolichucky
APPALACHIAN NATIONAL SCENIC TRAIL

Map Key

- ★ State capital
- ●●● City or town
- ---- National trail
- ····· State boundary
- National Park Service
- National Forest land

N

↑ The Grand Ole Opry in **Nashville** is the home of country music. Country music performers mainly use stringed instruments. This music form evolved from traditional folk tunes of the Appalachians.

← A male white-tailed deer with a full rack of antlers watches for danger in a meadow in **Great Smoky Mountains National Park.** The park is a popular vacation destination.

Virginia

Land & Water

The Blue Ridge mountains, Shenandoah National Park, and the James River are important land and water features of Virginia.

Statehood Virginia became the 10th state in 1788.

People & Places Virginia's population is 8,382,993. Richmond is the state capital. The largest city is Virginia Beach.

Fun Fact Eight U.S. presidents—Washington, Jefferson, Madison, Monroe, Harrison, Tyler, Taylor, and Wilson—were born in Virginia, more than in any other state.

↑ An old barn, bales of hay, and trees in autumn foliage are a common sight in the **Appalachian Mountains** of Virginia.

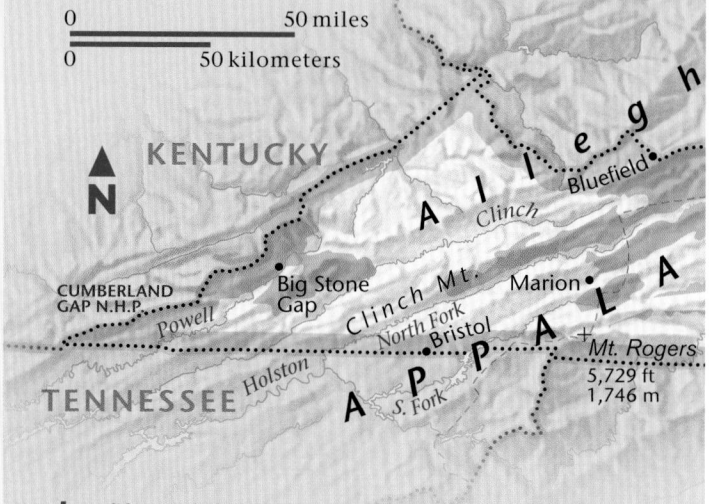

Virginia State Flag

Flowering Dogwood
State Flower

Cardinal
State Bird

↓ A fife and drum band maintains the tradition of military music as it marches down a street in **Williamsburg**, an early capital of Virginia.

Map Key
- ★ State capital
- ●●● City or town
- ■ Point of interest
- National trail
- State boundary
- Swamp
- National Park Service
- National Forest land

NEW JERSEY
MARYLAND
DELAWARE
DELMARVA PENINSULA
WEST VIRGINIA
VIRGINIA
NORTH CAROLINA
ATLANTIC OCEAN
Chesapeake Bay
Potomac
Rappahannock
Appomattox
James
York
Nottoway
Roanoke (Staunton)
Roanoke
New
Cowpasture
Shenandoah
Shenandoah Mountain
Blue Ridge Mountains
Appalachian Mountains
Potomac Trail
Lake Anna
Smith Mountain Lake
John H. Kerr Reservoir
Lake Gaston
Great Dismal Swamp
Highest point in Virginia
HARPERS FERRY N.H.P.
Winchester
Front Royal
LURAY CAVERNS
SHENANDOAH NATIONAL PARK
Luray
Harrisonburg
Leesburg
Reston
Arlington
D.C.
Alexandria
Manassas
Woodbridge
Culpeper
Fredericksburg
Charlottesville
Lexington
Richmond
Lynchburg
Roanoke
Blacksburg
Radford
Danville
Petersburg
COLONIAL N.H.P.
Williamsburg
Yorktown
Newport News
Hampton
Norfolk
Portsmouth
Chesapeake
Virginia Beach
Cape Charles
ASSATEAGUE ISLAND NATIONAL SEASHORE
Chincoteague

→ Winding under the Appalachian Mountains, **Luray Caverns** formed as water dissolved rocks, and the minerals dripped down to create stalactites and stalagmites.

← The sharp eyes of a great blue heron watch the water of a river near **Richmond** for a dinner of fish or frogs.

West Virginia

Land & Water

The Allegheny Mountains, Ohio River, and the New River are important land and water features of West Virginia.

Statehood West Virginia became the 35th state in 1863.

People & Places

West Virginia's population is 1,844,128. Charleston is the state capital and the largest city.

Fun Fact One of the oldest and largest Indian burial grounds is located in Moundsville along the Ohio River. It is more than 2,000 years old and 69 feet (21 m) high.

↑ West Virginia's rivers offer some of the best white-water rafting in the eastern United States. The **Gauley River** is called the Beast of the East.

← A coal miner's helmet recalls the history of mining in **West Virginia**. The state produced almost 12 percent of U.S. coal in 2012.

West Virginia State Flag

Rhododendron
State Flower

Cardinal
State Bird

↓ Trees turn red in the **Dolly Sods Wilderness** in the Monongahela National Forest. The area is named for an early settler family.

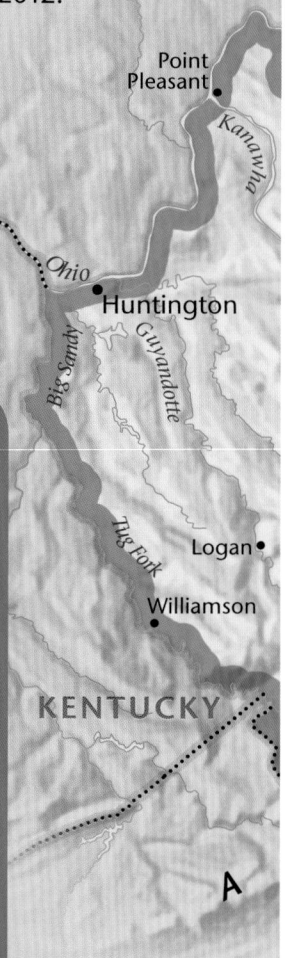

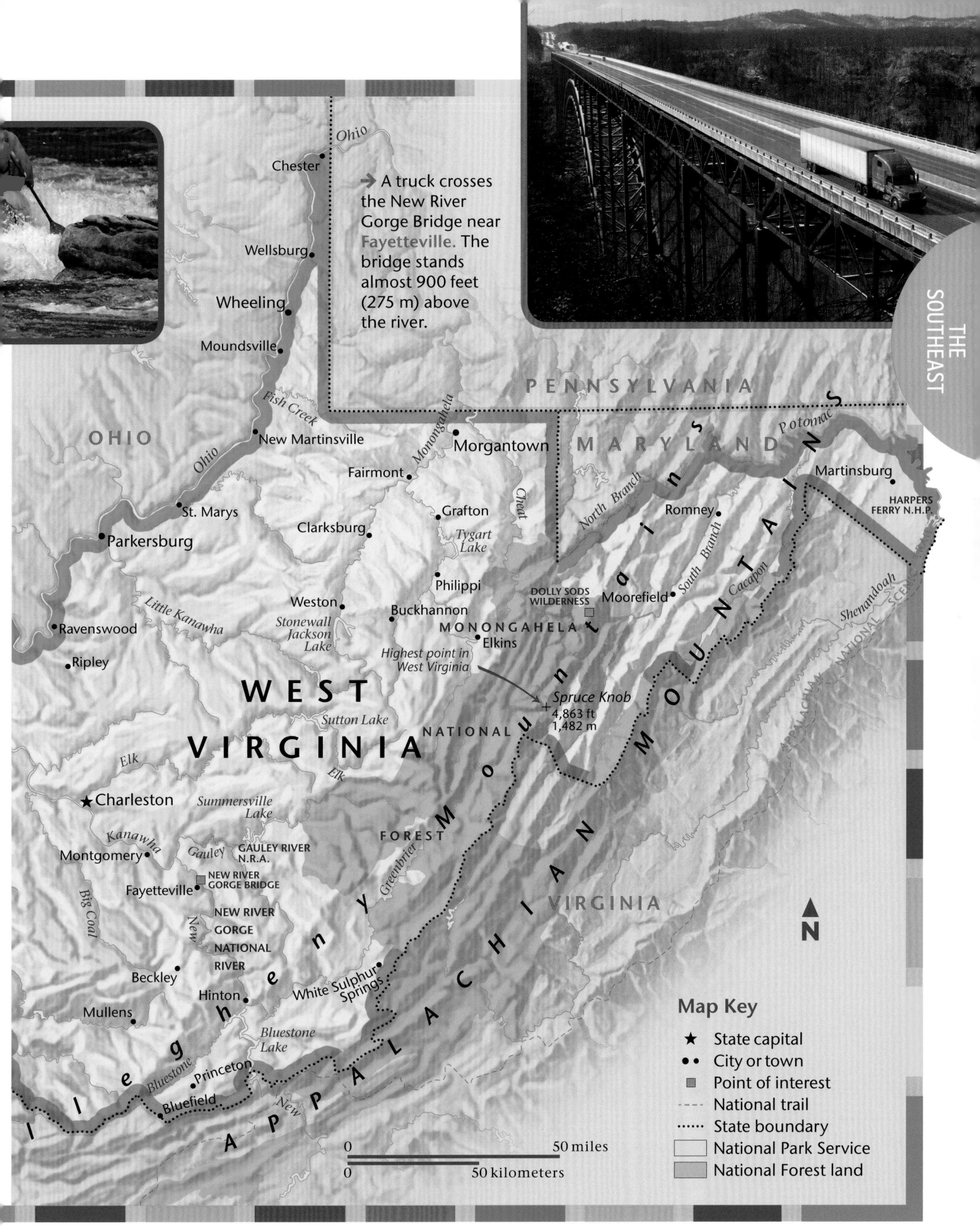
A truck crosses the New River Gorge Bridge near Fayetteville. The bridge stands almost 900 feet (275 m) above the river.
THE SOUTHEAST
Ohio
Chester
Wellsburg
Wheeling
Moundsville
Fish Creek
OHIO
New Martinsville
Ohio
Morgantown
Monongahela
PENNSYLVANIA
MARYLAND
Potomac
Fairmont
Martinsburg
HARPERS FERRY N.H.P.
St. Marys
Grafton
Cheat
North Branch
Romney
Parkersburg
Clarksburg
Tygart Lake
Philippi
South Branch
Cacapon
DOLLY SODS WILDERNESS
Moorefield
Weston
Buckhannon
Little Kanawha
Stonewall Jackson Lake
MONONGAHELA
Elkins
Ravenswood
Ripley
Highest point in West Virginia
Spruce Knob
4,863 ft
1,482 m
WEST VIRGINIA
Sutton Lake
NATIONAL
Elk
Elk
Charleston
Summersville Lake
Kanawha
Montgomery
Gauley
GAULEY RIVER N.R.A.
FOREST
Greenbrier
NEW RIVER GORGE BRIDGE
Fayetteville
Big Coal
New
NEW RIVER GORGE NATIONAL RIVER
VIRGINIA
Beckley
Hinton
White Sulphur Springs
Mullens
Bluestone Lake
Bluestone
Princeton
Bluefield
New
N
Map Key
State capital
City or town
Point of interest
National trail
State boundary
National Park Service
National Forest land
0
50 miles
0
50 kilometers

The Midwest

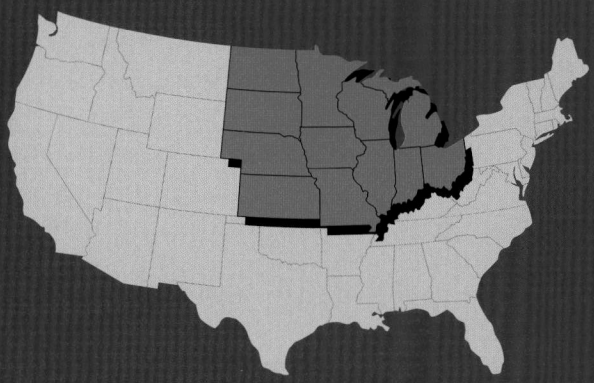

The Midwest is a region of glacier-carved lakes, mighty rivers, and rolling prairies. The Great Lakes are among the largest freshwater lakes in the world. The Mississippi River and its tributaries—the Missouri and the Ohio Rivers—drain America's heartland. The region's lowlands and plains support some of the most productive agriculture in the world. Industries such as food processing, steel, and automobile production supported the growth of cities such as Detroit, MI, Chicago, IL, and St. Louis, MO, but these industries are being replaced by businesses based on technology and information.

White clouds float across a blue sky above this flowering Kansas prairie. The Midwest is a major grain-producing region. Dairy cows are also an important part of the region's economy, supplying much of the country's milk, cheese, and butter.

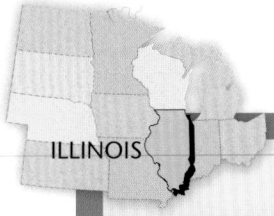

Illinois

Land & Water

The Shawnee National Forest, the Illinois River, and Lake Michigan are important land and water features of Illinois.

← Children ride bicycles along a sidewalk in Pilsen, on **Chicago**'s lower west side. A street mural celebrates the neighborhood's immigrant roots.

Statehood Illinois became the 21st state in 1818.

People & Places

Illinois has a population of 12,859,995. Springfield is the state capital. The largest city is Chicago.

Fun Fact A river that runs through Chicago is dyed green on St. Patrick's Day to honor the city's large Irish population. The formula for the green dye is a closely kept secret.

↑ Pig races are a fun-filled highlight of the annual Illinois State Fair in **Springfield.**

Illinois State Flag

Violet
State Flower

Cardinal
State Bird

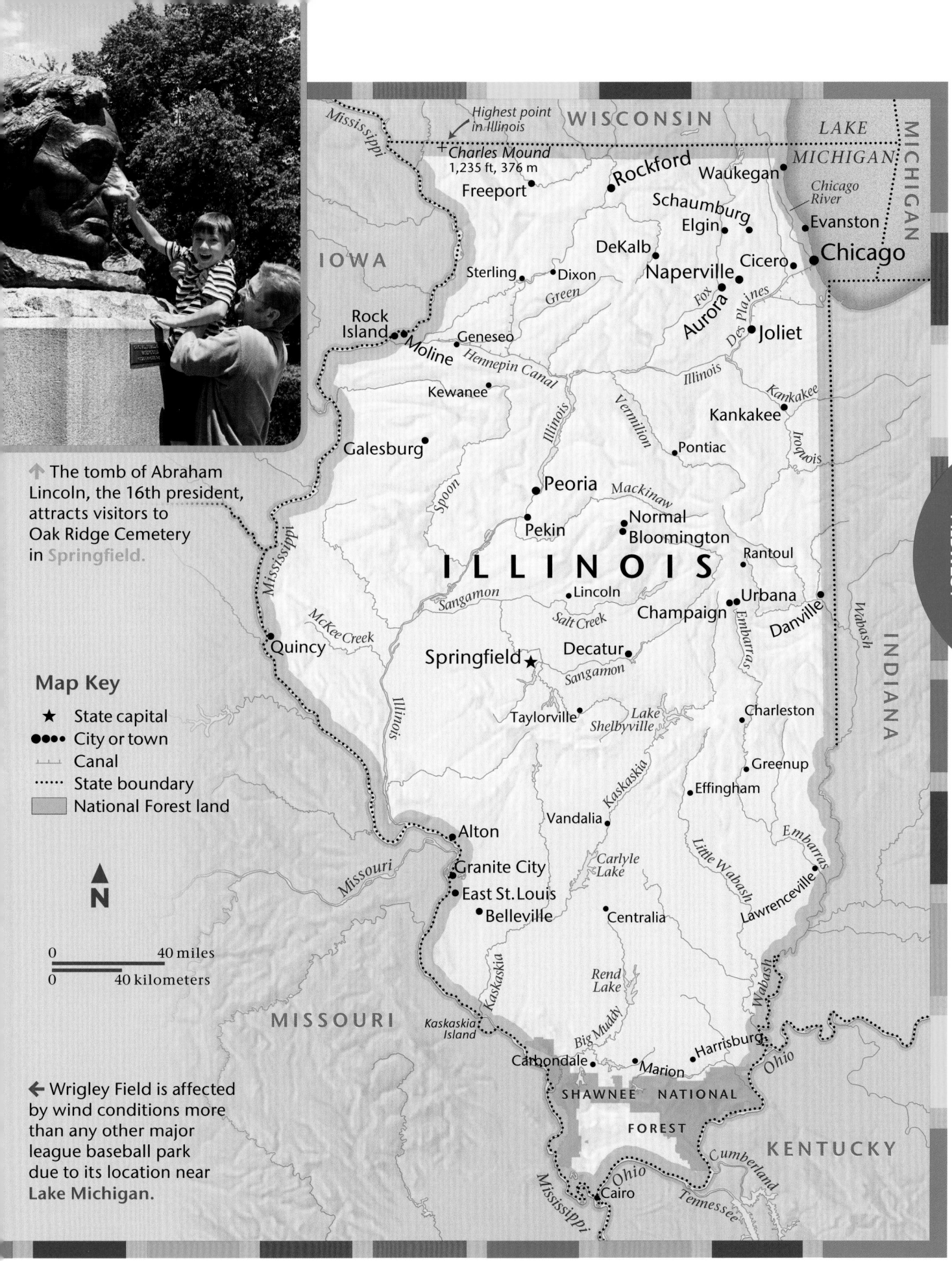

The tomb of Abraham Lincoln, the 16th president, attracts visitors to Oak Ridge Cemetery in **Springfield.**

Wrigley Field is affected by wind conditions more than any other major league baseball park due to its location near **Lake Michigan.**

THE MIDWEST

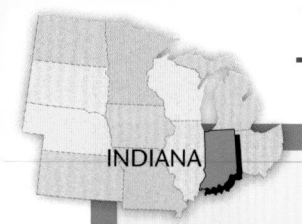

Indiana

Land & Water The Hoosier National Forest, Lake Michigan, and the Wabash River are important land and water features of Indiana.

Statehood Indiana became the 19th state in 1816.

People & Places Indiana's population is 6,619,680. Indianapolis is the state capital and the largest city.

Fun Fact The intersection of U.S. Highway 40 and U.S. Highway 41, at Wabash Avenue and Seventh Street in Terre Haute, is called the Crossroads of America.

↑ The **Indianapolis** Motor Speedway is the largest sports stadium in the world. It seats 250,000 and hosts the famous Indy 500.

→ The Hoosiers of Indiana University, located in **Bloomington,** are a part of college football's powerful Big Ten Conference. Sports are an important tradition and a favorite pastime in Indiana.

Indiana State Flag

Peony
State Flower

Cardinal
State Bird

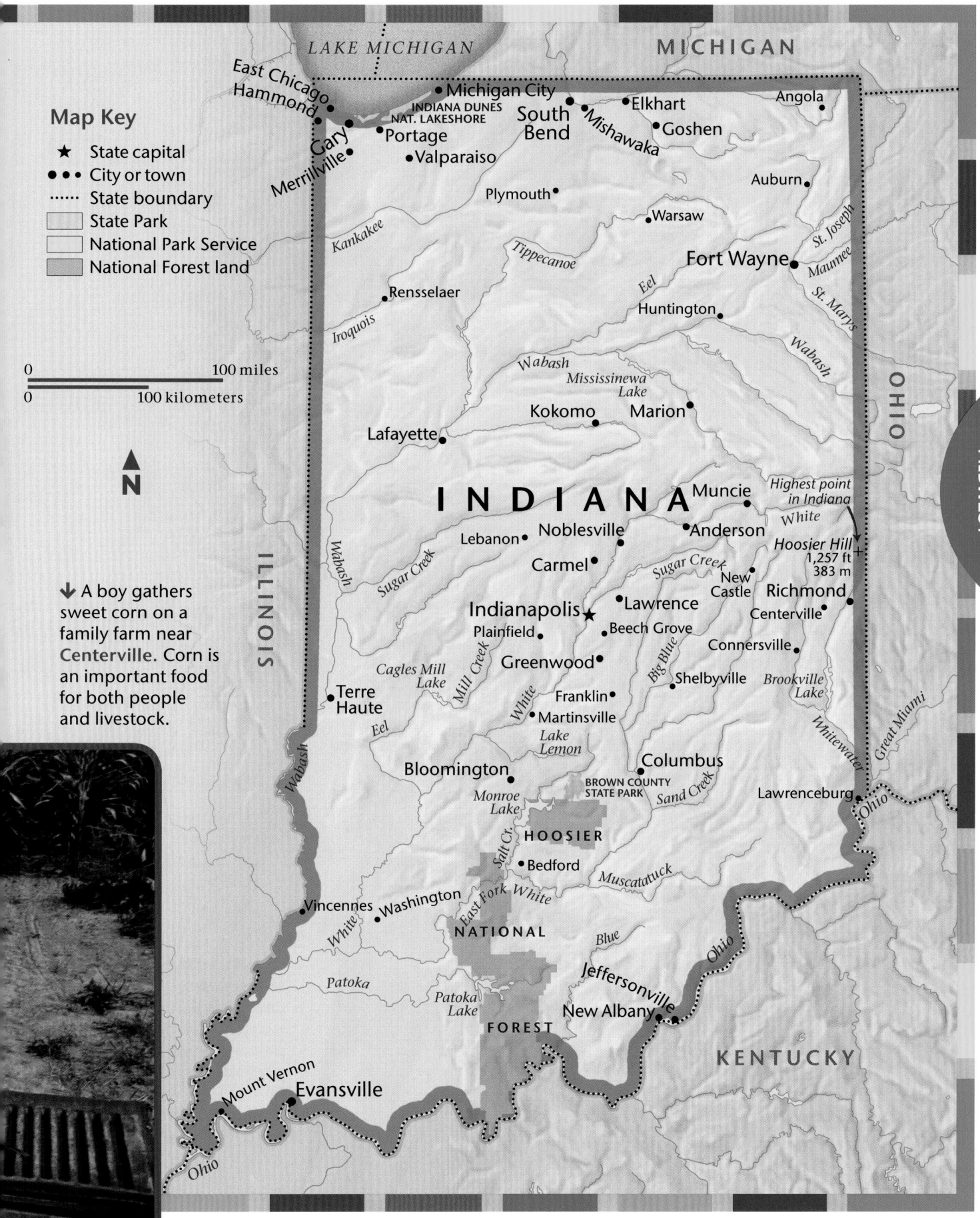

A boy gathers sweet corn on a family farm near **Centerville.** Corn is an important food for both people and livestock.

THE MIDWEST

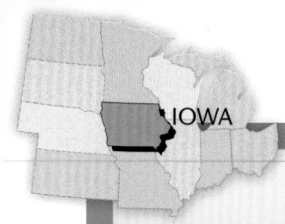

Iowa

Land & Water Hawkeye Point and the Missouri and Mississippi Rivers are important land and water features of Iowa.

Statehood Iowa became the 29th state in 1846.

People & Places Iowa's population is 3,123,899. Des Moines is the state capital and the largest city.

Fun Fact Iowa's nickname, the Hawkeye State, comes from Chief Black Hawk, the Sauk Indian chief who started the Black Hawk War in 1832.

↑ Hogs outnumber people almost seven to one in Iowa, which produces nearly one-third of all hogs raised in the United States.

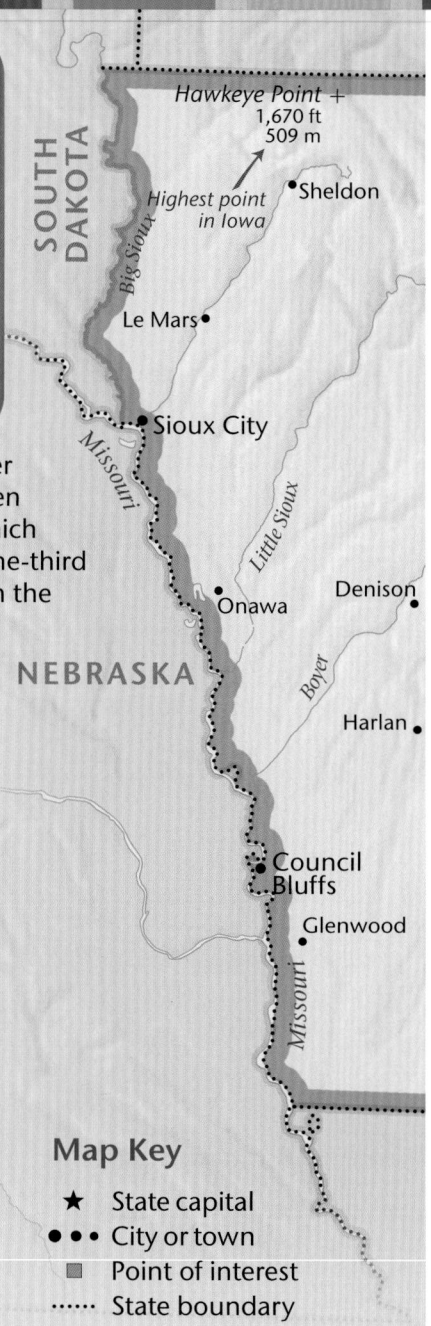

Map Key

- ★ State capital
- ●●● City or town
- ■ Point of interest
- ····· State boundary

Iowa State Flag

Wild Rose
State Flower

American Goldfinch
State Bird

← A young Native American boy dressed in colorful traditional clothing prepares to participate in the Annual Meskwaki Powwow near Tama.

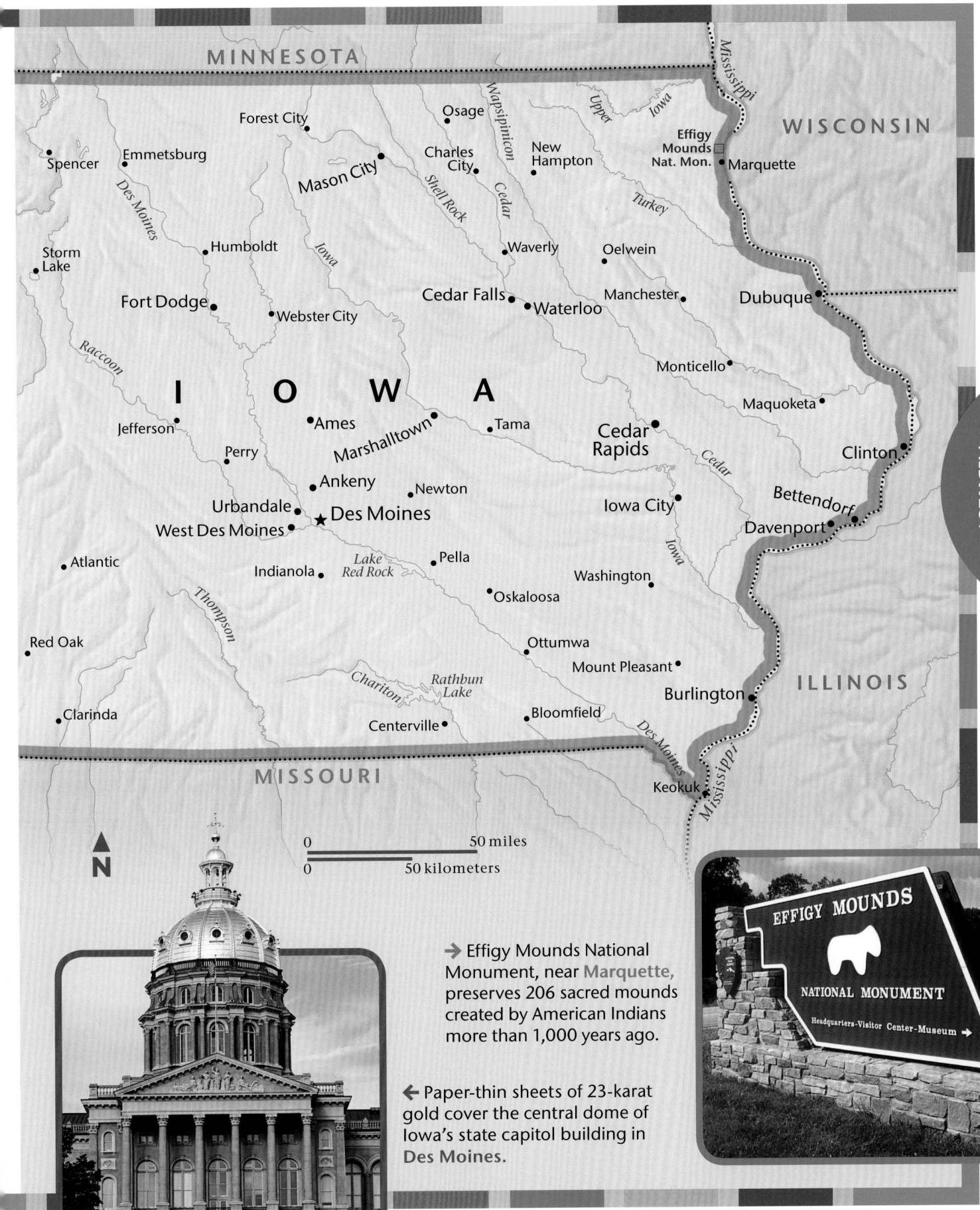

→ Effigy Mounds National Monument, near **Marquette,** preserves 206 sacred mounds created by American Indians more than 1,000 years ago.

← Paper-thin sheets of 23-karat gold cover the central dome of Iowa's state capitol building in **Des Moines.**

Kansas

Land & Water Mount Sunflower, the Flint Hills, and the Missouri River are important land and water features of Kansas.

Statehood Kansas became the 34th state in 1861.

People & Places The population of Kansas is 2,911,641. Topeka is the state capital. The largest city is Wichita.

Fun Fact Pizza Hut, the world's largest pizza chain, opened its first restaurant in Wichita in 1958. Today the company has branches in more than 100 countries.

↑ A statue of the Tin Man, a character from *The Wonderful Wizard of Oz,* the popular fantasy book partly set in Kansas, sits in a garden.

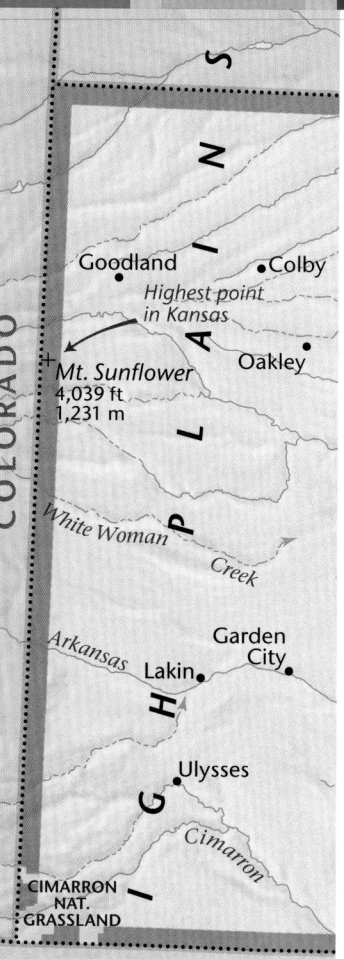

Map Key

- ★ State capital
- ●●● City or town
- ····· State boundary
- Indian Reservation
- National Park Service
- National Grassland

Kansas State Flag

Western Meadowlark
State Bird

Sunflower
State Flower

↓ Monument Rocks, located south of Oakley, were once part of an ancient inland sea bed. Over millions of years, erosion by wind and water has created these chalk formations.

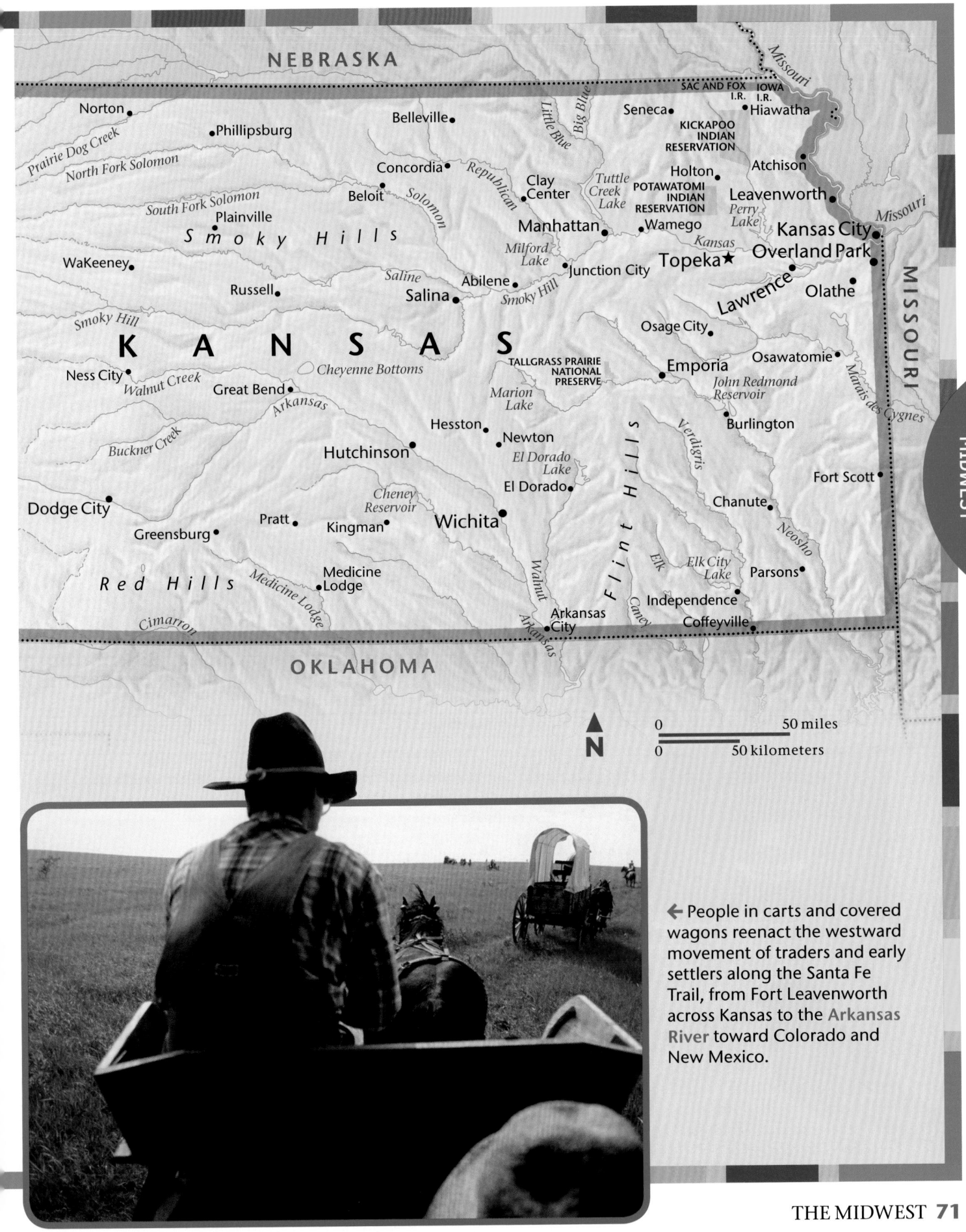

← People in carts and covered wagons reenact the westward movement of traders and early settlers along the Santa Fe Trail, from Fort Leavenworth across Kansas to the **Arkansas River** toward Colorado and New Mexico.

Michigan

Land & Water The Upper and Lower Peninsulas and Lakes Superior, Michigan, and Huron are important land and water features of Michigan.

Statehood Michigan became the 26th state in 1837.

People & Places Michigan's population is 9,922,576. Lansing is the state capital. The largest city is Detroit.

Fun Fact The record company Motown, named for Detroit's nickname Motor City, grew from a small start-up business in 1959 to one of the largest independent record companies in the world.

← A statue of Austin Blair, governor of Michigan during the Civil War, stands in front of the state capitol in **Lansing.**

← Boys explore nature's wonders on the bank of a river near **Niles.** The town sits on the site of Fort St. Joseph, built by the French in 1691.

Michigan State Flag

Apple Blossom
State Flower

Robin
State Bird

↓ The Straits of Mackinac join Lakes Michigan and Huron. Crossing the straits, the five-mile (8-km)-long Mackinac Bridge connects Michigan's **Upper Peninsula** to the southern part of the state.

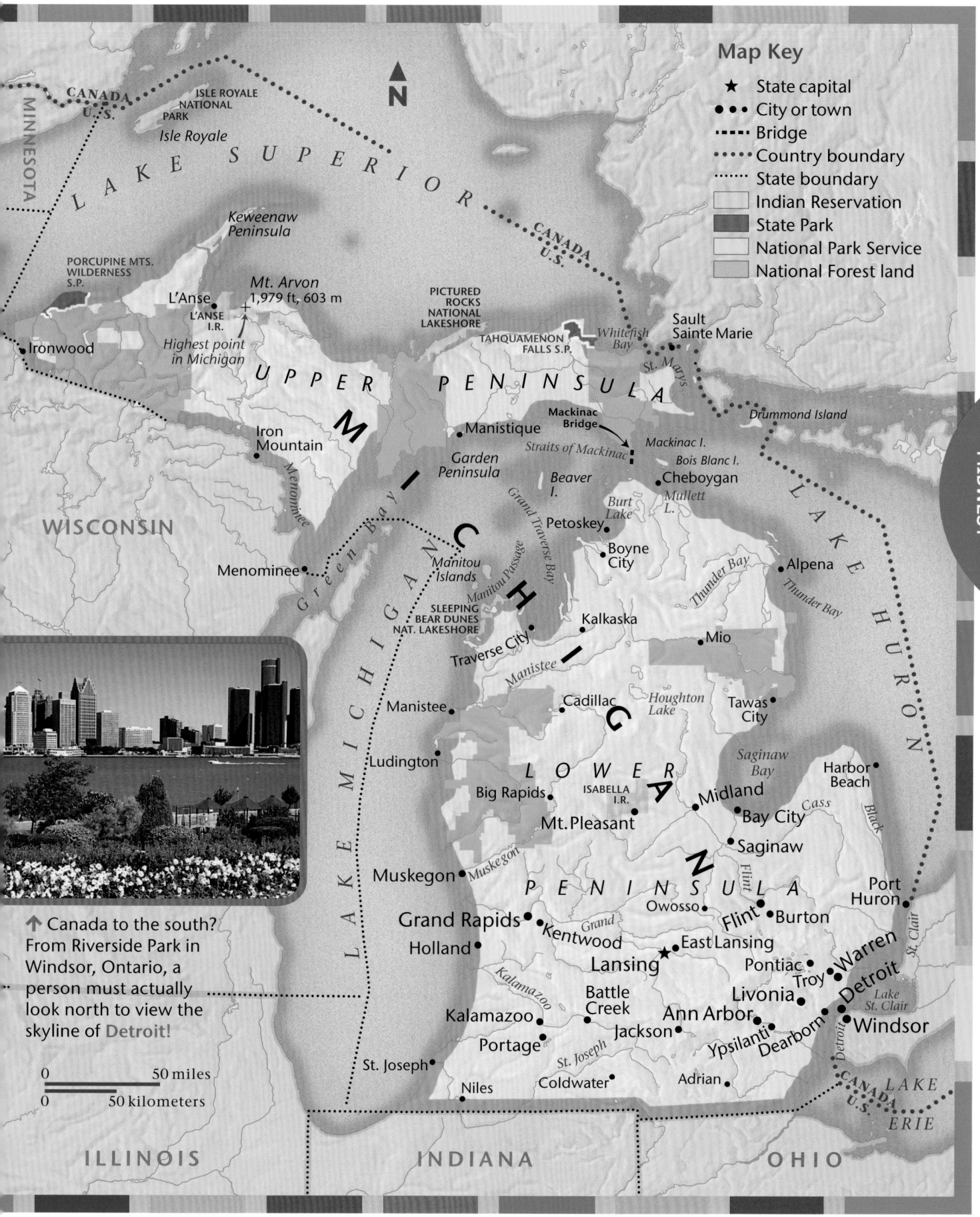

↑ Canada to the south? From Riverside Park in Windsor, Ontario, a person must actually look north to view the skyline of **Detroit!**

THE MIDWEST

Minnesota

Land & Water Chippewa National Forest, Lake Superior, and the Mississippi River are important land and water features of Minnesota.

Statehood Minnesota became the 32nd state in 1858.

People & Places Minnesota's population is 5,489,594. St. Paul is the state capital. The largest city is Minneapolis.

Fun Fact Modern in-line skates were invented by two Minnesota students. Looking for a way to practice hockey in the summer, they replaced their skate blades with wheels.

← Minnesota's gray wolf population is growing and no longer endangered thanks to the work of the International Wolf Center in Ely.

↓ Some people in Minnesota sit for hours in "ice shacks" and fish through holes cut in the ice of frozen lakes.

Minnesota State Flag

Showy Lady's Slipper
State Flower

Common Loon
State Bird

← The skyline of Minneapolis rises above Lake Harriet, part of a popular recreation area called Chain of Lakes.

↑ A young woman wearing the traditional dress of an Indian princess prepares to join the dancing at the Minneapolis Powwow.

Missouri

Land & Water Mark Twain National Forest and the Missouri and Mississippi Rivers are important land and water features of Missouri.

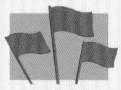

Statehood Missouri became the 24th state in 1821.

People & Places Missouri's population is 6,083,672. Jefferson City is the state capital. The largest city is Kansas City.

Fun Fact Mark Twain's childhood in Hannibal, a town on the Mississippi River, inspired many of his books, including *The Adventures of Tom Sawyer* and *The Adventures of Huckleberry Finn*.

↑ In 2004 St. Charles celebrated the bicentennial of the Lewis and Clark expedition, which explored the northwestern part of the Louisiana Purchase. The historic journey began in Missouri.

Missouri State Flag

Eastern Bluebird
State Bird

Hawthorn
State Flower

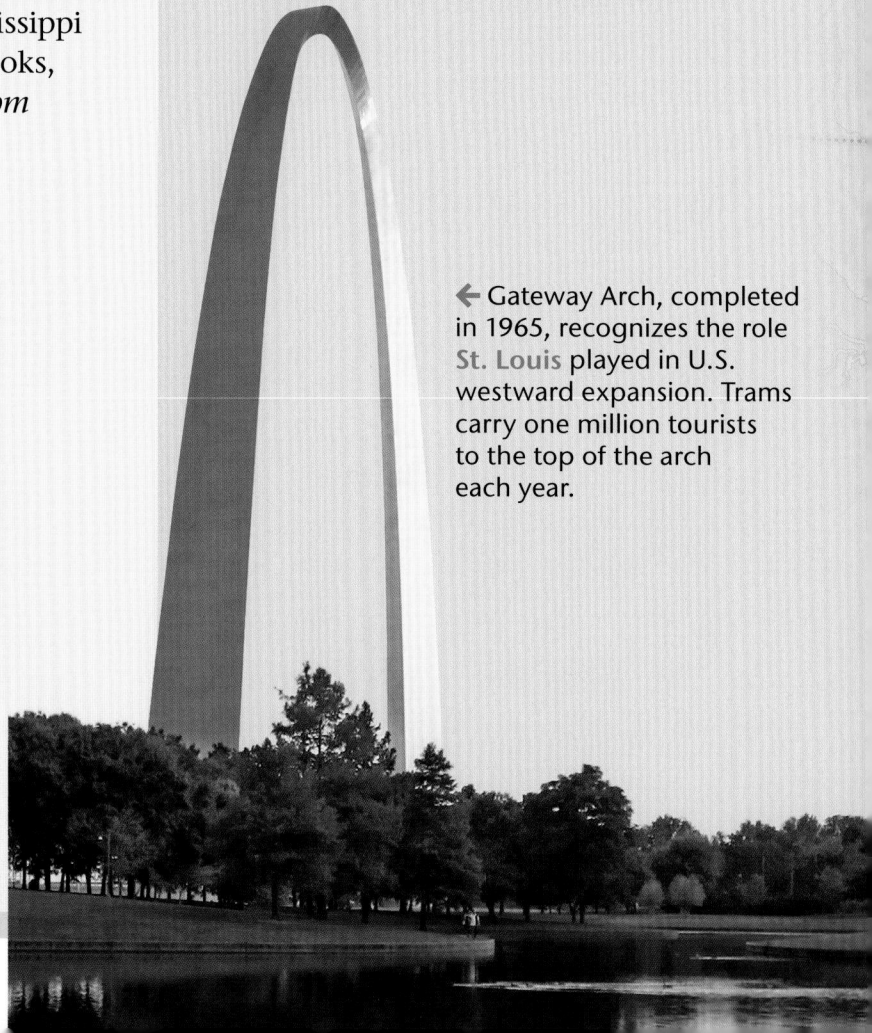

← Gateway Arch, completed in 1965, recognizes the role St. Louis played in U.S. westward expansion. Trams carry one million tourists to the top of the arch each year.

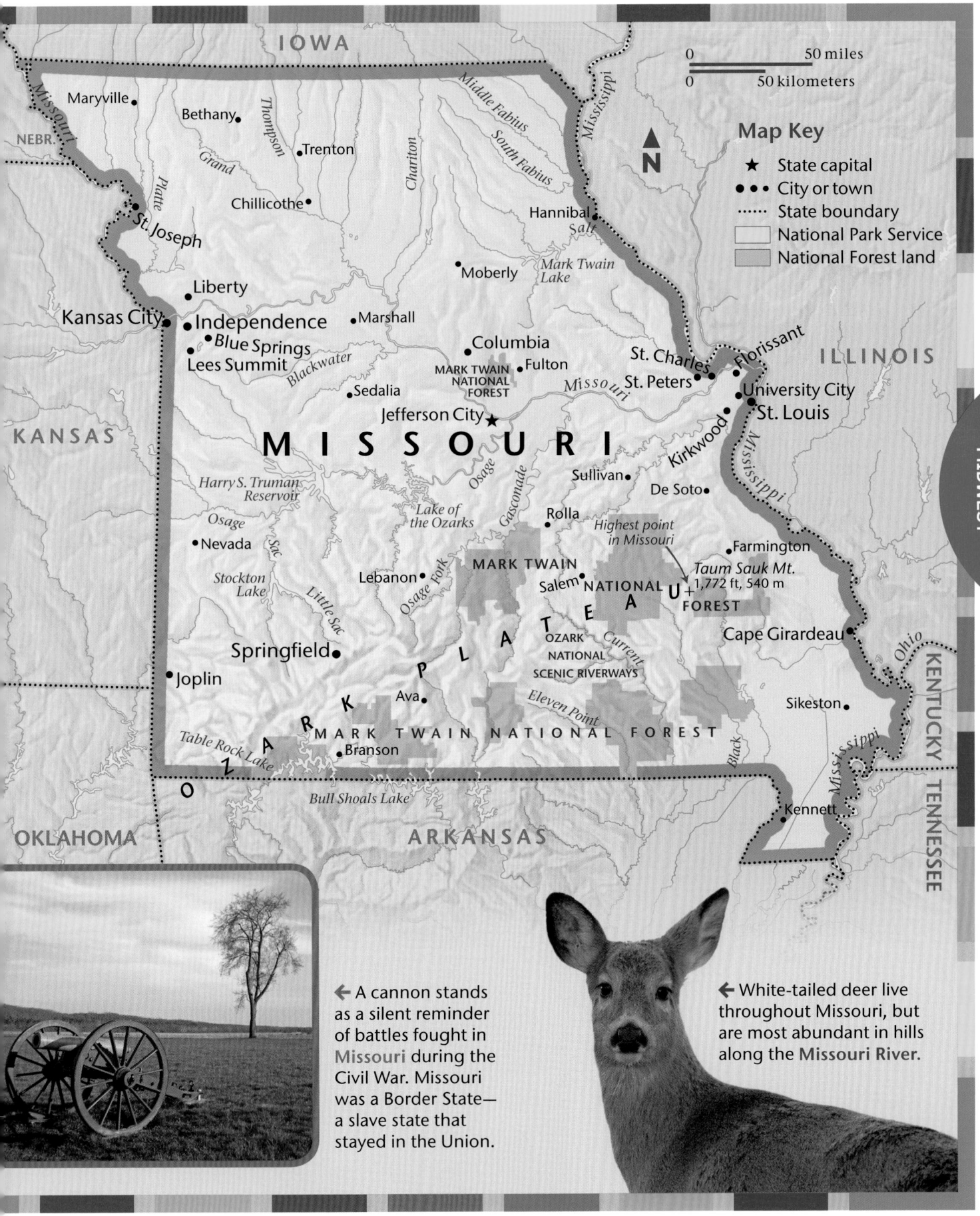

← A cannon stands as a silent reminder of battles fought in **Missouri** during the Civil War. Missouri was a Border State—a slave state that stayed in the Union.

← White-tailed deer live throughout Missouri, but are most abundant in hills along the **Missouri River.**

Nebraska

Land & Water The Sand Hills and the Platte and Missouri Rivers are important land and water features of Nebraska.

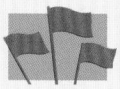

Statehood Nebraska became the 37th state in 1867.

People & Places Nebraska's population is 1,896,190. Lincoln is the state capital. The largest city is Omaha.

Fun Fact The largest remaining area of original native prairie in the United States is in the Sand Hills region. It is an important stopover for migrating sandhill cranes.

← Two black-tailed prairie dogs watch for signs of danger at the entrance to their burrow in the **Fort Niobrara National Wildlife Refuge.**

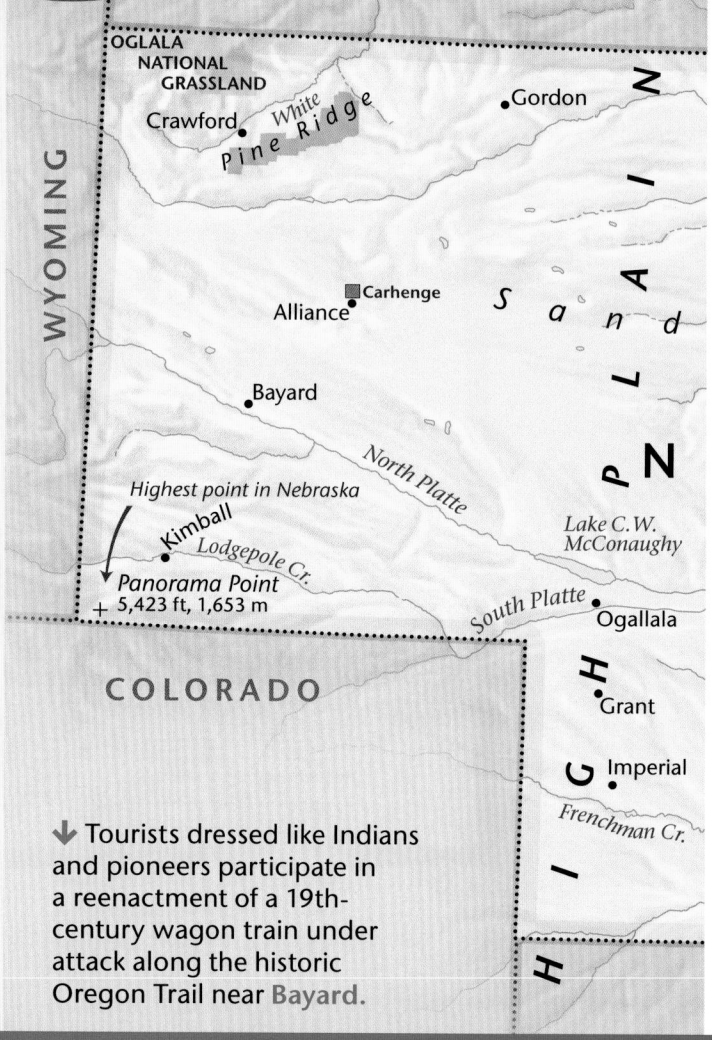

Nebraska State Flag

Goldenrod
State Flower

Western Meadowlark
State Bird

↓ Tourists dressed like Indians and pioneers participate in a reenactment of a 19th-century wagon train under attack along the historic Oregon Trail near **Bayard.**

↑ In recent years annual snowfall in Lincoln has averaged about 25 inches (64 cm), creating work for adults but fun for kids.

→ Carhenge, near Alliance, is a sculpture made out of old cars that are painted gray and designed to look like Stonehenge, which is a famous archaeological site in southern England.

North Dakota

Land & Water The Badlands, the Red River of the North, and the Missouri River are important land and water features of North Dakota.

Statehood North Dakota became the 39th state in 1889.

People & Places North Dakota's population is 756,927. Bismarck is the state capital. The largest city is Fargo.

Fun Fact North Dakota leads the United States in honey production, with more than 33 million pounds (14 million kg) produced annually. In addition to honey, bees produce wax and help pollinate crops.

↑ Fossils of prehistoric life, such as this leaf, can be found in **North Dakota**'s sedimentary rock formations.

↑ Cowboys on the fence watch the excitement of the rodeo during the Slope County Fair in **Amidon.**

North Dakota State Flag

Wild Prairie Rose
State Flower

Western Meadowlark
State Bird

← American bison are native to the Great Plains, but now they are found mainly in parks such as **Sullys Hill National Game Preserve.**

CANADA
U.S.
MONTANA
Williston
Missouri
LITTLE
Watford City
THEODORE ROOSEVELT N.P. (NORTH UNIT)
Little Missouri
Yellowstone
MISSOURI
Theodore Roosevelt N.P. (Elkhorn Ranch Site)
Badlands
NATIONAL
THEODORE ROOSEVELT N.P. (SOUTH UNIT)
Medora
GRASSLAND
Amidon
White Butte
3,506 ft
1,069 m
Highest point in North Dakota
Cedar
Little Missouri
Hettinger
0 100 miles
0 100 kilometers
N

CANADA
U.S.
Turtle Mts.
TURTLE MT. I.R.
Rolla
Pembina
Langdon
Souris
GREAT PLAINS
Drift Prairie
Cando
Towner
Souris (Mouse)
Minot
New Town
FORT BERTHOLD INDIAN RESERVATION
Lake Sakakawea
Sullys Hill National Game Preserve
Devils Lake
SPIRIT LAKE SIOUX I.R.
Grand Forks
Sheyenne
Harvey
James
Northwood
Garrison
Audubon Lake
New Rockford
Red River of the North
MINNESOTA
NORTH DAKOTA
Hillsboro
Washburn
Beulah
Knife
Missouri
Pipestem Creek
Center
Fargo
Valley City
Mandan
Bismarck
Jamestown
West Fargo
Long Lake
Maple
Heart
James
Sheyenne
Lake Oahe
SHEYENNE NATIONAL GRASSLAND
Mott
LaMoure
Wahpeton
Cannonball
Wishek
Wild Rice
Maple
STANDING ROCK INDIAN RESERVATION
Creek
CEDAR RIVER NATIONAL GRASSLAND
Fort Yates
Ellendale
Oakes
LAKE TRAVERSE (SISSETON) INDIAN RESERVATION
SOUTH DAKOTA

Map Key

- ★ State capital
- •• City or town
- ■ Point of interest
- •••• Country boundary
- ····· State boundary
- Indian Reservation
- National Park Service
- National Grassland

← Painted Canyon stretches as far as the eye can see in **Theodore Roosevelt National Park.** The park is a living memorial to the 26th president and home to many animal species, from wild horses to snapping turtles.

Ohio

Land & Water Wayne National Forest, Lake Erie, and the Ohio River are important land and water features of Ohio.

Statehood Ohio became the 17th state in 1803.

People & Places Ohio's population is 11,613,423. Columbus is the state capital and the largest city.

Fun Fact Ohio's nickname, the Buckeye State, comes from a local tree. The tree's name was derived from Native Americans, who thought its seeds looked like the eye of a male deer, or buck.

↑ Fourth of July fireworks light up the nighttime sky above **Columbus.** The city has been the state capital since 1816.

↑ Colorful guitars mark the entrance to the Rock and Roll Hall of Fame, established in downtown **Cleveland** in 1995.

Ohio State Flag

Scarlet Carnation
State Flower

Cardinal
State Bird

↓ The Blue Streak is the oldest operating roller coaster at Cedar Point Amusement Park in **Sandusky.** This popular ride is named after a local high school sports team.

→ Horse-drawn buggies are a familiar sight in **Ohio**, home to the world's largest Amish population.

South Dakota

Land & Water The Black Hills, Buffalo Gap National Grassland, and the Missouri River are important land and water features of South Dakota.

Statehood South Dakota became the 40th state in 1889.

People & Places South Dakota's population is 858,469. Pierre is the state capital. The largest city is Sioux Falls.

Fun Fact A dinosaur nicknamed Sue was unearthed on the Cheyenne River Indian Reservation in 1990. It is the world's largest, most complete, and best preserved specimen of a *Tyrannosaurus rex*.

↑ A mountain cottontail nibbles on some grass in **Wind Cave National Park.**

← Widespread dinosaur fossils in **South Dakota** prompted this humorous sign.

South Dakota State Flag

Pasqueflower
State Flower

Ring-Necked Pheasant
State Bird

MONTANA
WYOMING
Little Missouri
GRAND RIVER
S. Fork Grand
Buffalo
North Fork
South Fork
Sulphur Creek
Belle Fourche
Sturgis
Deadwood
Belle Fourche
Black Hills
Rapid City
Highest point in South Dakota
Harney Peak
7,242 ft
2,207 m
Mount Rushmore N.M.
CUSTER S.P.
WIND CAVE N.P.
Hot Springs
Edgemont
Cheyenne
BUFFALO GAP NATIONAL
BADLANDS N.P.
PINE INDIAN
White
Pine Ridge
N
0 50 miles
0 50 kilometers

↓ Carvings on **Mount Rushmore** in the Black Hills honor four past presidents (from left to right): George Washington, Thomas Jefferson, Theodore Roosevelt, and Abraham Lincoln.

NORTH DAKOTA
STANDING ROCK INDIAN RESERVATION
McIntosh
Missouri
Grand
NAT. GRASSLAND
Bison
Timber Lake
Moreau
CHEYENNE RIVER INDIAN RESERVATION
Cherry Creek
Cheyenne
Eureka
Selby
Ipswich
Aberdeen
Groton
James
Coteau des Prairies
LAKE TRAVERSE INDIAN RES.
Sisseton
Lake Traverse
Big Stone Lake
Milbank
MINNESOTA
Watertown
Big Sioux
Lake Poinsett
Lake Oahe
Gettysburg
Faulkton
Okobojo Creek
Onida
GREAT PLAINS
SOUTH DAKOTA
Fort Pierre
Pierre
Missouri
Huron
Brookings
FORT PIERRE NATIONAL GRASSLAND
CROW CREEK IND. RES.
Lake Sharpe
LOWER BRULE IND. RES.
Fort Thompson
Crow Cr.
Wessington Springs
Madison
Philip
Bad
GRASSLAND
Kadoka
Kennebec
BADLANDS N.P.
White
Chamberlain
Mitchell
Sioux Falls
PINE RIDGE I.R.
ROSEBUD INDIAN RESERVATION
White River
Little White
RIDGE RES.
Winner
Lake Francis Case
Platte
Parkston
James
YANKTON INDIAN RES.
Wagner
Martin
Keya Paha
Lewis and Clark Lake
Big Sioux
IOWA
NEBRASKA
Missouri

Map Key

- ★ State capital
- ●●● City or town
- ■ Point of interest
- ····· State boundary
- Indian Reservation
- State Park
- National Park Service
- National Forest land
- National Grassland

← Young people ride their horses past a tipi on the **Pine Ridge Indian Reservation.** The reservation is home to almost 17,000 members of the Oglala Sioux, people who are part of the Lakota Nation.

Wisconsin

Land & Water The Door Peninsula and Lakes Superior and Michigan are important land and water features of Wisconsin.

Statehood Wisconsin became the 30th state in 1848.

People & Places Wisconsin's population is 5,771,337. Madison is the state capital. The largest city is Milwaukee.

Fun Fact Laura Ingalls Wilder was born in Pepin in 1867. Her famous Little House books are based on her childhood in the forests and prairies of the Midwest.

↑ In **Wisconsin** bald eagles are found only in the northern regions.

← A young Native American man in colorful traditional dress dances at a festival in **Milwaukee.**

↑ In a winter version of sailing, ice boats compete in a race on the frozen surface of **Lake Winnebago** near Oshkosh.

Wisconsin State Flag

Robin
State Bird

Wood Violet
State Flower

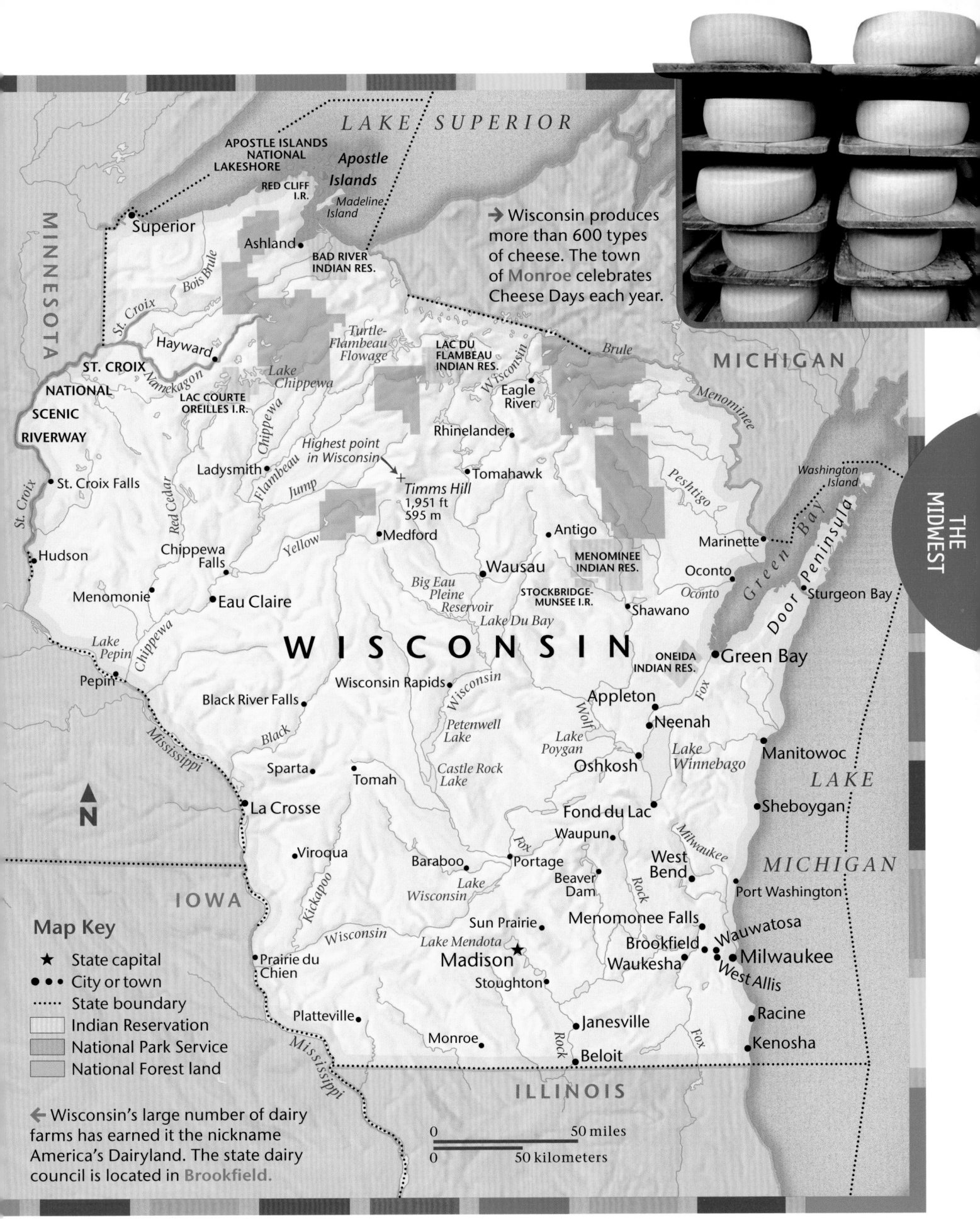

→ Wisconsin produces more than 600 types of cheese. The town of **Monroe** celebrates Cheese Days each year.

← Wisconsin's large number of dairy farms has earned it the nickname America's Dairyland. The state dairy council is located in **Brookfield**.

The Southwest

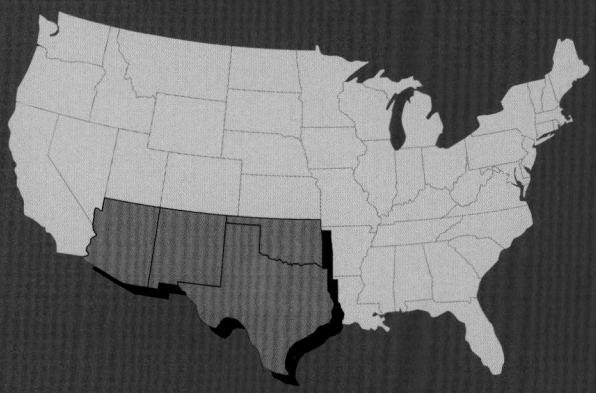

The Southwest region extends from the humid Gulf Coast in the east to the arid canyonlands in the west. The people of the region are just as varied as the natural landscape. Native Americans, descendants of early Spanish settlers, and recent immigrants from Mexico and Central America contribute to this region's special cultural landscape. Agriculture, cattle ranching, and the oil industry are traditional economic activities. The Southwest is part of the Sunbelt, where rapid population growth and sprawling cities are putting pressure on the region's limited water resources.

A rainbow frames Big Bend National Park's Cerro Castellon, in Texas. This eroded mount of volcanic rock rises almost 3,300 feet (1,006 m) above the desert floor. Raising horses is a part of the cultural tradition in this region.

Arizona

Land & Water The Colorado Plateau, the Grand Canyon, and the Colorado River are important land and water features of Arizona.

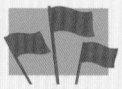

Statehood Arizona became the 48th state in 1912.

People & Places Arizona's population is 6,828,065. Phoenix is the state capital and the largest city.

Fun Fact Of the 21 Indian reservations in Arizona, the largest belongs to the Navajo Nation. Native peoples and the federal government own 70 percent of the state's land area.

↑ Daring boaters get soaked as they run the rapids on the fast-flowing waters of the **Colorado River** in Grand Canyon National Park.

↓ Saguaro cactus, found in the **Sonoran Desert**, can grow more than 30 feet (9 m) tall.

Arizona State Flag

Cactus Wren
State Bird

Saguaro
State Flower

← Native American dancers perform in the Parada del Sol in **Scottsdale.** This monthlong celebration ends with rodeos and a grand parade.

New Mexico

Land & Water The Sangre de Cristo Mountains, Carlsbad Caverns, and the Rio Grande are important land and water features of New Mexico.

Statehood New Mexico became the 47th state in 1912.

People & Places New Mexico's population is 2,085,109. Santa Fe is the state capital. The largest city is Albuquerque.

Fun Fact Roswell is a popular destination for people interested in UFOs. A local rancher discovered what he believed to be wreckage of a UFO in 1947.

↑ Brightly colored hot-air balloons rise into a blue sky above **Albuquerque** during the International Balloon Fiesta, the largest such event in the world.

← The caves of **Carlsbad Caverns** were created as natural sulfuric acid dissolved the limestone rocks.

New Mexico State Flag

Yucca
State Flower

Roadrunner
State Bird

↓ Chili peppers, seen here in a store in **Santa Fe**, give Southwestern food a distinctive taste. New Mexico is second only to California in the production of chilies.

UTAH
COLORADO
OKLA.
TEXAS
ARIZONA
NEW MEXICO
Only spot in the U.S. where the borders of four states come together
FOUR CORNERS
NAVAJO NATION
UTE MOUNTAIN UTE I.R.
San Juan
Navajo Reservoir
Aztec
Farmington
Shiprock
JICARILLA APACHE INDIAN RESERVATION
Chama
Rio Grande
Sangre de Cristo Mts.
Wheeler Peak
13,161 ft, 4,011 m
TAOS PUEBLO
Taos
Highest point in New Mexico
Springer
Canadian
Clayton
KIOWA AND RITA BLANCA NATIONAL GRASSLANDS
Ute Creek
Navajo
CHACO CULTURE N.H.P.
Continental Divide
Chimayo
SANTA CLARA PUEBLO
Los Alamos
NAMBE PUEBLO
JEMEZ PUEBLO
BANDELIER N.M.
Santa Fe
COCHITI PUEBLO
SANTO DOMINGO PUEBLO
SAN FELIPE PUEBLO
ZIA PUEBLO
Las Vegas
Conchas Lake
Gallup
LAGUNA PUEBLO
SANTA ANA PUEBLO
Bernalillo
SANDIA I.R.
TO'HAJILEE NAVAJO I.R.
Rio Rancho
Albuquerque
Conchas
Tucumcari
Zuni
ZUNI I.R.
RAMAH NAVAJO IND. RES.
EL MALPAIS N.M.
ACOMA PUEBLO
LAGUNA PUEBLO
Rio San Jose
ISLETA PUEBLO
Los Lunas
Pecos
Santa Rosa
Rio Puerco
ALAMO NAVAJO I.R.
Mountainair
Fort Sumner
Clovis
Socorro
Reserve
San Francisco
Black Range
Truth or Consequences
San Andres Mountains
Sacramento Mountains
Carrizozo
Roswell
Rio Hondo
LLANO ESTACADO
MESCALERO APACHE INDIAN RES.
Alamogordo
WHITE SANDS N.M.
Silver City
Gila
Continental Divide
Hobbs
Guadalupe Mts.
Carlsbad
CARLSBAD CAVERNS N.P.
Las Cruces
Anthony
Sunland Park
U.S. MEXICO
Map Key
State capital
City or town
Point of interest
Country boundary
State boundary
Continental Divide
Indian Reservation
National Park Service
National Forest land
National Grassland
N
0 50 miles
0 50 kilometers

Oklahoma

Land & Water Black Mesa, the Ouachita Mountains, and the Arkansas River are important land and water features of Oklahoma.

Statehood Oklahoma became the 46th state in 1907.

People & Places Oklahoma's population is 3,911,338. Oklahoma City is the state capital and the largest city.

Fun Fact Before it became a state, Oklahoma was known as Indian Territory. Today 39 Indian nations, including the Cherokee, Creek, Osage, and Choctaw, have their headquarters in the state.

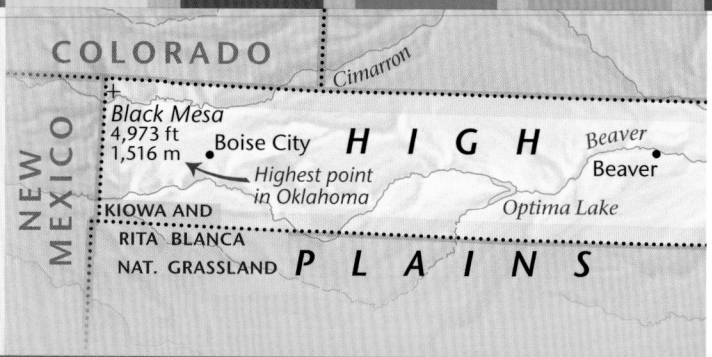

↑ A tornado is a destructive rotating column of air that forms from a thunderstorm. In 1974 five tornadoes struck **Oklahoma City** in one day.

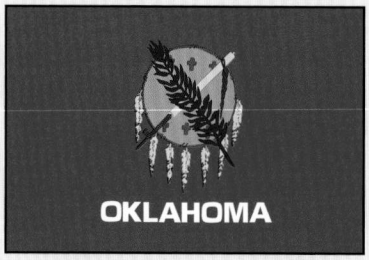

Oklahoma State Flag

Mistletoe
State Flower

Scissor-Tailed Flycatcher
State Bird

↑ The Golden Driller, with his hand on an oil rig, stands 76 feet (23 m) tall near the State Fairgrounds in **Tulsa.**

KANSAS
MISSOURI
ARKANSAS
TEXAS
OKLAHOMA
OSAGE NATION INDIAN RES.
OZARK PLATEAU
BLACK KETTLE NATIONAL GRASSLAND
Ouachita Mountains
Wichita Mts.
Arbuckle Mts.
CHICKASAW N.R.A.
Buffalo
Woodward
Fairview
Enid
Stillwater
Ponca City
Kaw Lake
Great Salt Plains Lake
Salt Fork
Rock Creek
Sooner Lake
North Canadian
Cimarron
Canadian
Keystone Lake
Pawhuska
Bartlesville
Verdigris
Vinita
Miami
Lake O' The Cherokees
Oologah Lake
Skiatook Lake
Owasso
Tulsa
Broken Arrow
Bixby
Pryor
Lake Hudson
Ft. Gibson Lake
Illinois
Tahlequah
Muskogee
Okmulgee
Tenkiller Lake
Sallisaw
Arkansas
Robert S. Kerr Lake
Poteau
Heavener
McAlester
Sardis Lake
Kiamichi
Broken Bow Lake
Hugo
Hugo Lake
Idabel
Red
Edmond
El Reno
Oklahoma City
Deep Fork
Clinton
Washita
Sayre
North Fork
Elm Fork
Mangum
Hollis
Salt Fork
Prairie Dog Town Fork
Hobart
Anadarko
Chickasha
Norman
Moore
Shawnee
Little
Seminole
N. Canadian
Eufaula Lake
Purcell
Lawton
Pauls Valley
Ada
Sulphur
Duncan
Frederick
Walters
Ardmore
Lake Texoma
Durant
McGee Cr. Lake
Atoka

N
0 50 miles
0 50 kilometers

Map Key

- ★ State capital
- ●●● City or town
- ····· State boundary
- Indian Reservation
- National Park Service
- National Forest land
- National Grassland

← Young girls wearing traditional dress reflect the strong Native American heritage in **Oklahoma.**

→ The collared lizard is Oklahoma's state reptile. The lizard is common in the **Wichita Mountains** and throughout the state.

Texas

Land & Water The Edwards Plateau, Padre Island National Seashore, and the Rio Grande are important land and water features of Texas.

Statehood Texas became the 28th state in 1845.

People & Places The population of Texas is 27,469,114. Austin is the state capital. The largest city is Houston.

Fun Fact Over the course of its history, six different national flags have flown over Texas—Spanish, French, Mexican, Texan, Confederate, and American.

Texas State Flag

↑ The brightly lit Congress Avenue Bridge crosses Town Lake into downtown **Austin**, where tall buildings rise against the night sky.

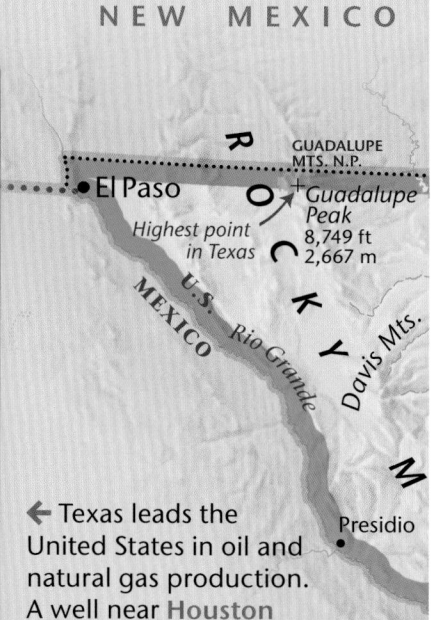

← Texas leads the United States in oil and natural gas production. A well near **Houston** pumps oil, called "black gold" because it's worth so much money.

Mockingbird
State Bird

Bluebonnet
State Flower

↓ The colorful coach whip snake is found in western **Texas.** It can grow up to six feet (1.8 m) long.

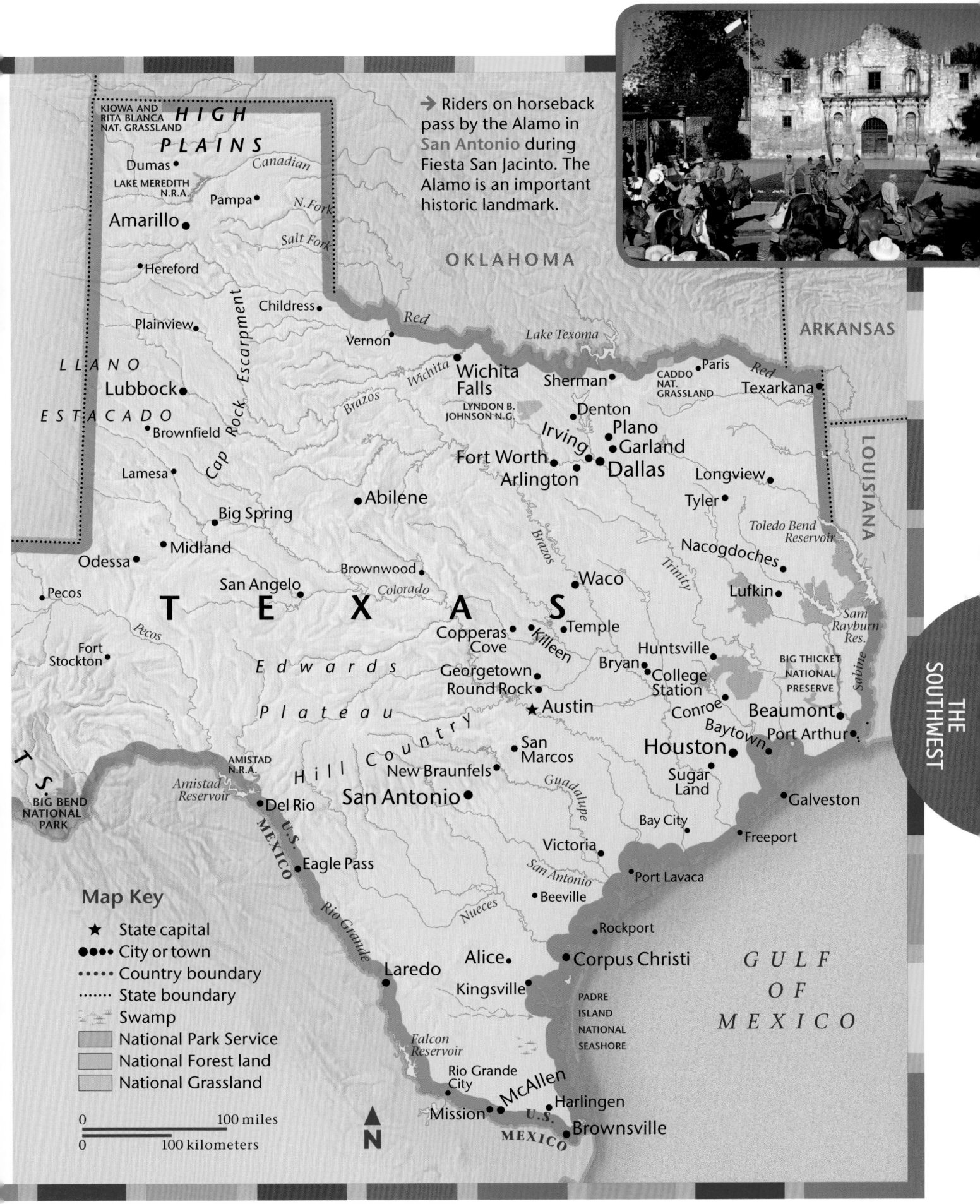

→ Riders on horseback pass by the Alamo in **San Antonio** during Fiesta San Jacinto. The Alamo is an important historic landmark.

The West

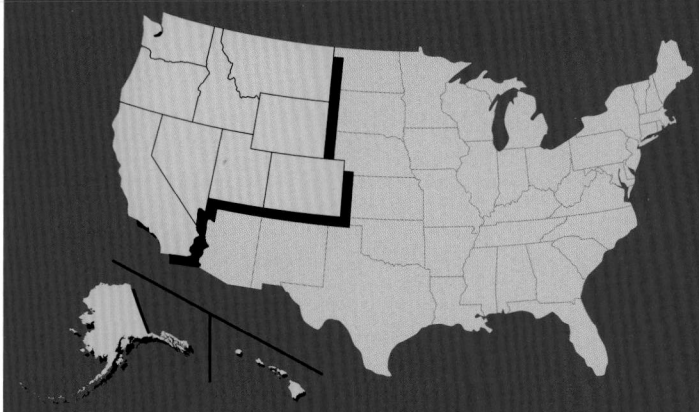

The West region makes up almost half of the landmass of the United States. The region's varied landscapes and climates range from the frozen heights of Denali in Alaska, to the barren desert of Death Valley in California and the lush tropical forests of Hawai'i. More than half the population lives in California. The Los Angeles metropolitan area is second in size only to that of New York City. Other parts of the region have few people, and much of the land is set aside as parkland and military bases.

The snowy peaks of Maroon Bells–Snowmass Wilderness near Aspen, Colorado, rise over 14,000 feet (4,200 m). Mountains—the Rockies, Tetons, and Sierra Nevadas—are important landscape features of the West and provide habitat for mountain lions (right) and other wildlife.

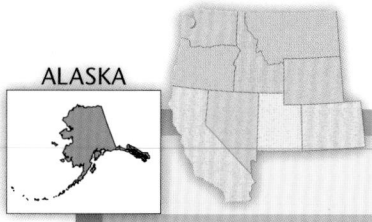

Alaska

Land & Water The Tongass National Forest, Brooks Range, and the Yukon River are important land and water features of Alaska.

Statehood Alaska became the 49th state in 1959.

People & Places Alaska's population is 738,432. Juneau is the state capital. The largest city is Anchorage.

Fun Fact The most powerful earthquake ever recorded in North America struck Anchorage in 1964. Eighty times more powerful than the 1906 San Francisco earthquake, it measured 9.2 on the Richter scale.

Alaska State Flag

Forget-Me-Not
State Flower

Willow Ptarmigan
State Bird

↑ Dogsledding has a long and colorful history in Alaska. The most famous race is the Iditarod, which runs from Anchorage to **Nome** along an old mail and supply route.

← Native peoples in Alaska carved totem poles to tell their histories. Carvers still make totem poles at Saxman Native Village in **Ketchikan**.

CHUKCHI

RUSSIA

Bering

St. Lawrence I.

St. Matthew I.

Nunivak I.

BERING SEA

St. Paul

Pribilof Islands

ALEUTIAN ISLANDS

Unimak I.

Unalaska I.

Umnak I.

Unalaska

Islands of Four Mountains

Yunaska I.

Continuation of the Aleutian Islands on map to the right

PACIFIC OCEAN

Many types of crabs are found in Alaska. Golden king crabs live in waters around the Aleutian Islands in southwest Alaska.

THE WEST

California

Land & Water The Sierra Nevada, Death Valley, and San Francisco Bay are important land and water features of California.

Statehood California became the 31st state in 1850.

People & Places California's population is 39,144,818. Sacramento is the state capital. The largest city is Los Angeles.

Fun Fact Death Valley is the hottest place in the United States. In July 1913 what is now Furnace Creek Ranch registered a temperature of 134°F (57°C).

→ Stretching more than a mile (1.6 km) across the entrance to **San Francisco Bay,** the Golden Gate Bridge opened in 1937.

↑ An elephant seal on one of California's **Channel Islands** roars at a photographer who has invaded the seal's territory on the beach.

California State Flag

Golden Poppy
State Flower

California Quail
State Bird

↓ In **Leggett,** automobiles can drive through the base of this redwood tree, nicknamed the Chandelier Tree because of its huge branches.

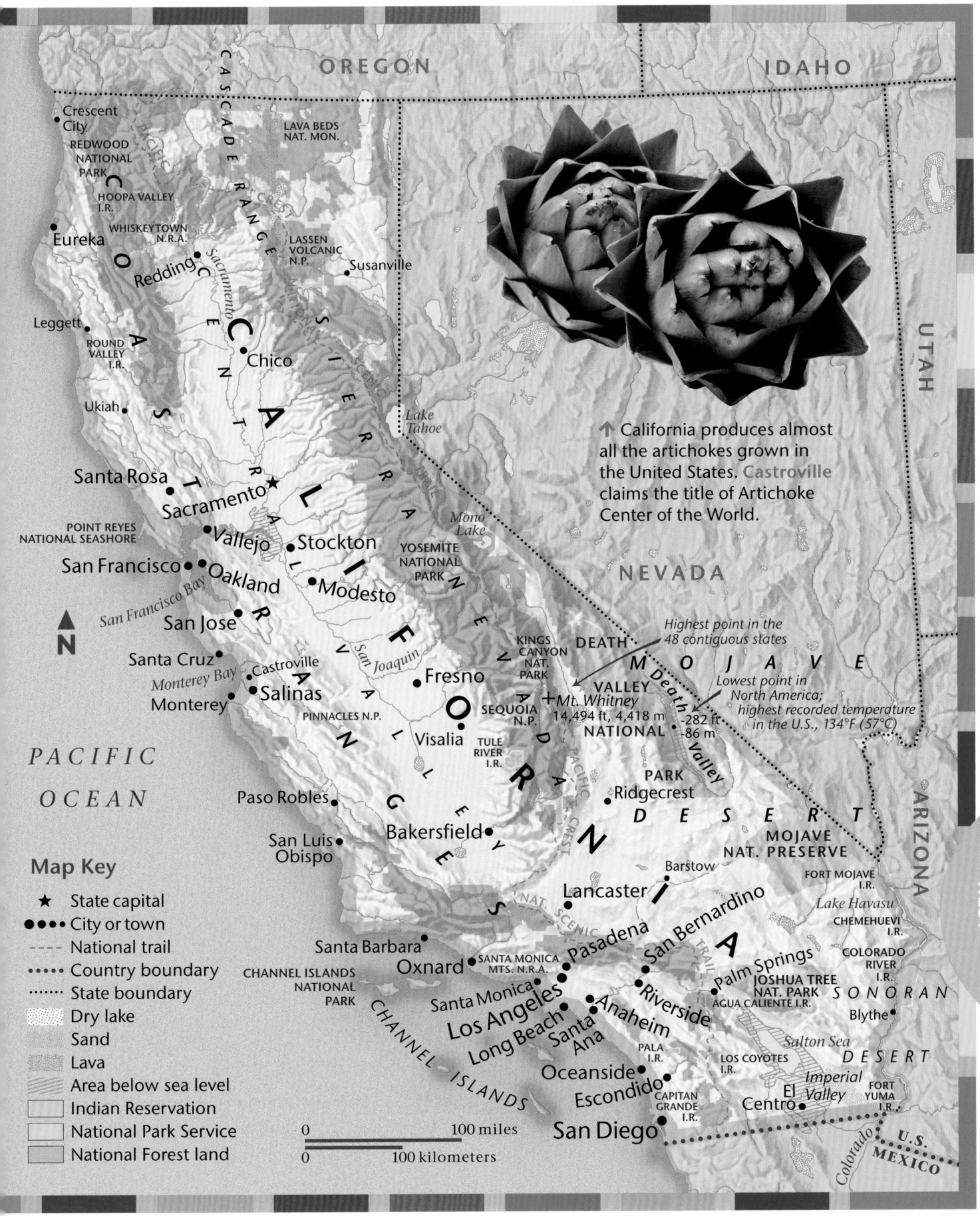

California produces almost all the artichokes grown in the United States. **Castroville** claims the title of Artichoke Center of the World.

Colorado

Land & Water The Rocky Mountains, Roosevelt National Forest, and the Colorado River are important land and water features of Colorado.

Statehood Colorado became the 38th state in 1876.

People & Places Colorado's population is 5,456,574. Denver is the state capital and the largest city.

Fun Fact The 700-foot (210-m)-high sand dunes in Great Sand Dunes National Park and Preserve occupy an area that was covered by an ancient sea more than a million years ago.

↑ Bighorn sheep, known for their large curled horns, live in **Rocky Mountain National Park** and other mountainous areas of the West.

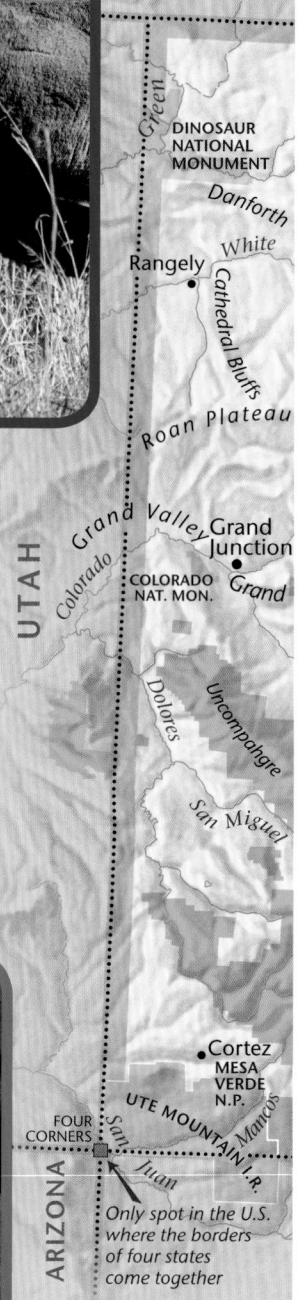

↓ Early native people built more than 600 stone structures into cliff walls that are now part of **Mesa Verde National Park.**

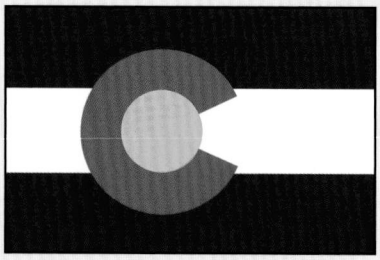

Colorado State Flag

Columbine
State Flower

Lark Bunting
State Bird

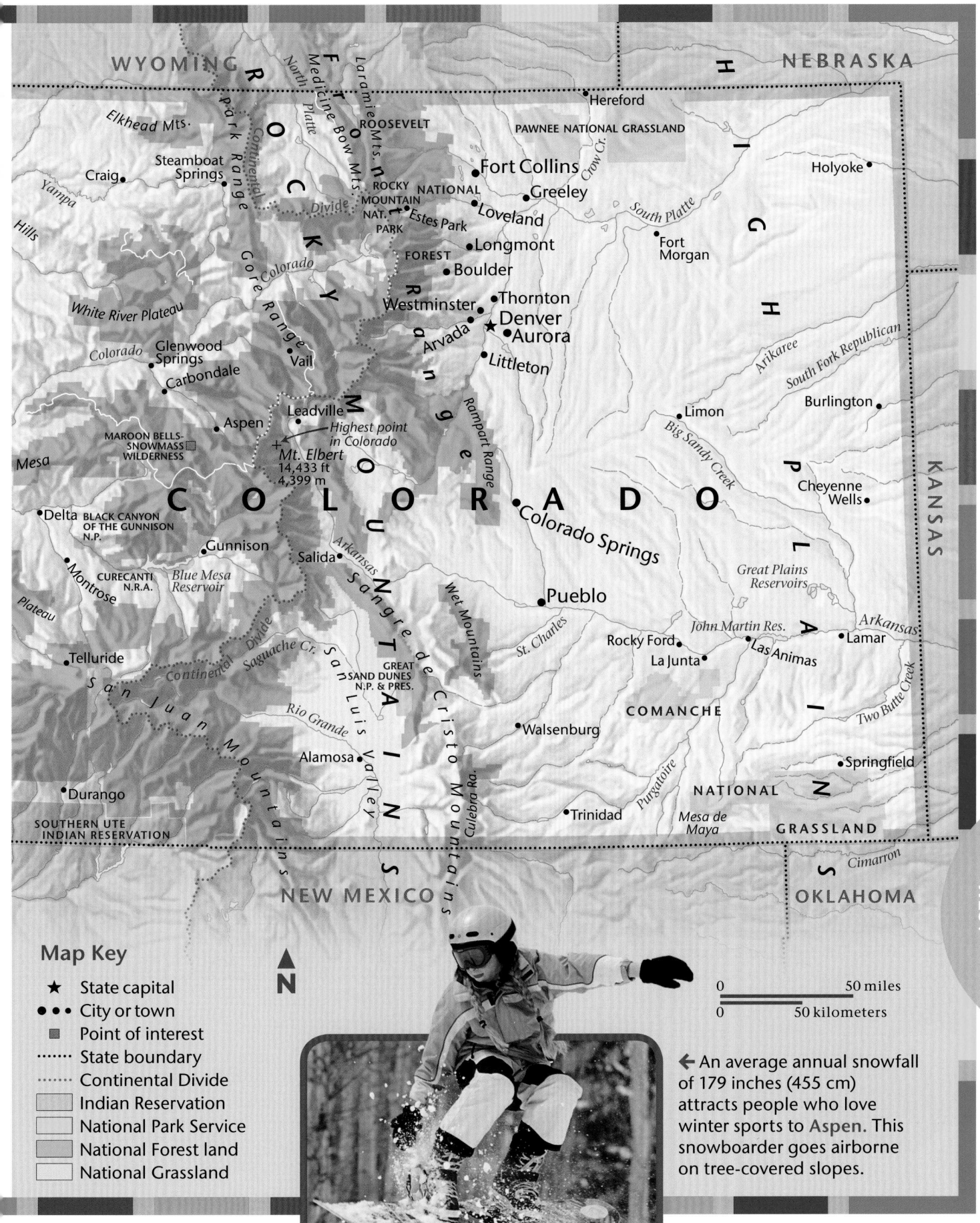

← An average annual snowfall of 179 inches (455 cm) attracts people who love winter sports to **Aspen**. This snowboarder goes airborne on tree-covered slopes.

Hawai'i

Land & Water Kilauea crater, Diamond Head, and Pearl Harbor are important land and water features of Hawai'i.

Statehood Hawai'i became the 50th state in 1959.

People & Places Hawai'i's population is 1,431,603. Honolulu is the state capital and the largest city.

Fun Fact Hawai'i is the fastest growing state in the United States—not in people, but in land. Active volcanoes are constantly creating new land as lava flows into the sea.

← Pu'u 'Ō'ō vent on **Kilauea crater** has added more than 568 acres (230 ha) of new land to Hawai'i.

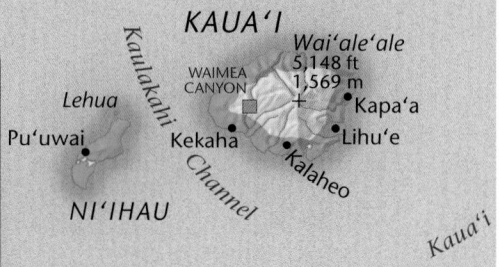

Hawai'i State Flag

Hibiscus
State Flower

Hawaiian Goose (Nene)
State Bird

↓ Hawai'i is the leading pineapple producer in the United States. Pineapples are grown on **Lāna'i**, **Maui**, and **O'ahu**.

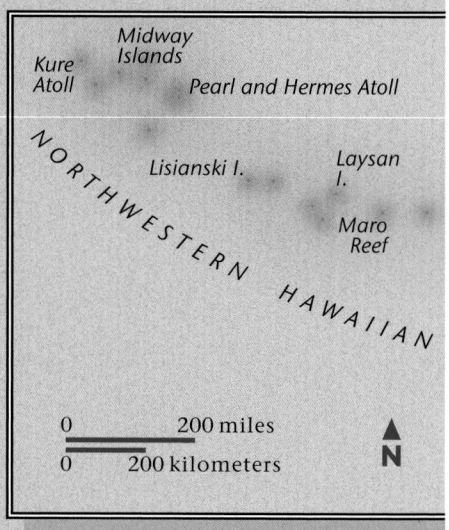

← A surfer balances on his board. People travel great distances to ride the big waves off the North Shore of **O'ahu.**

→ A young girl performs a traditional Polynesian hula on a misty day in Waimea Canyon on the island of **Kaua'i.**

→ Green sea turtles migrate 800 miles (1,287 km) to their nesting area in the **Northwestern Hawaiian Islands.**

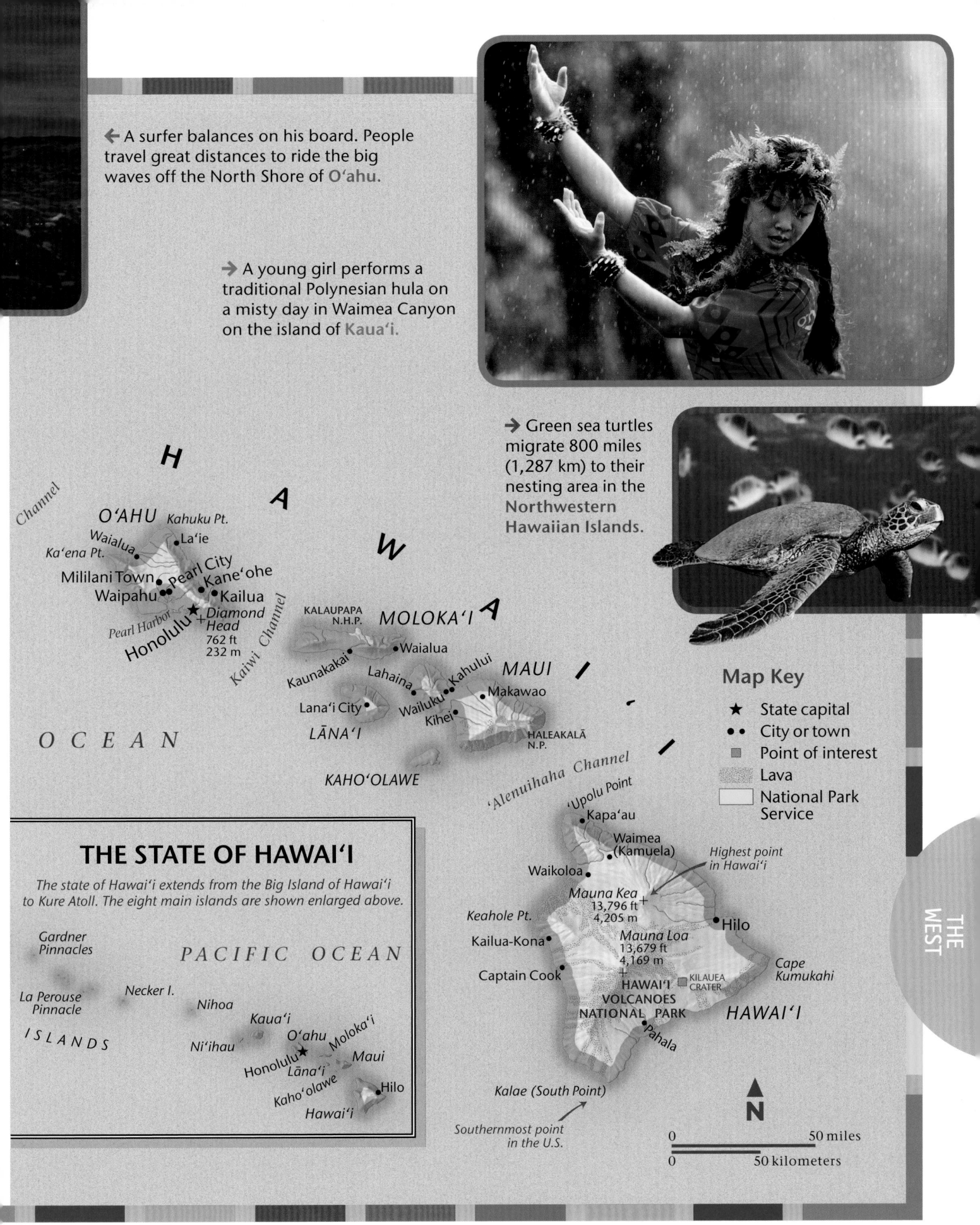

Idaho

Land & Water The Bitterroot Range, the Columbia Plateau, and the Snake River are important land and water features of Idaho.

Statehood Idaho became the 43rd state in 1890.

People & Places Idaho's population is 1,654,930. Boise is the state capital and the largest city.

Fun Fact In preparation for their mission to the moon, American astronauts visited Craters of the Moon National Monument and Preserve to study its volcanic geology and experience its harsh environment.

↑ A wood duck perches on a post. These colorful waterfowl can be viewed in Kootenai National Wildlife Refuge near **Bonners Ferry.**

↑ More than 40 percent of Idaho's land area is forested. Use of this land is overseen by the Forest Products Commission in **Boise.** Forest products are important to the state's economy.

Idaho State Flag

Syringa (Mock Orange)
State Flower

Mountain Bluebird
State Bird

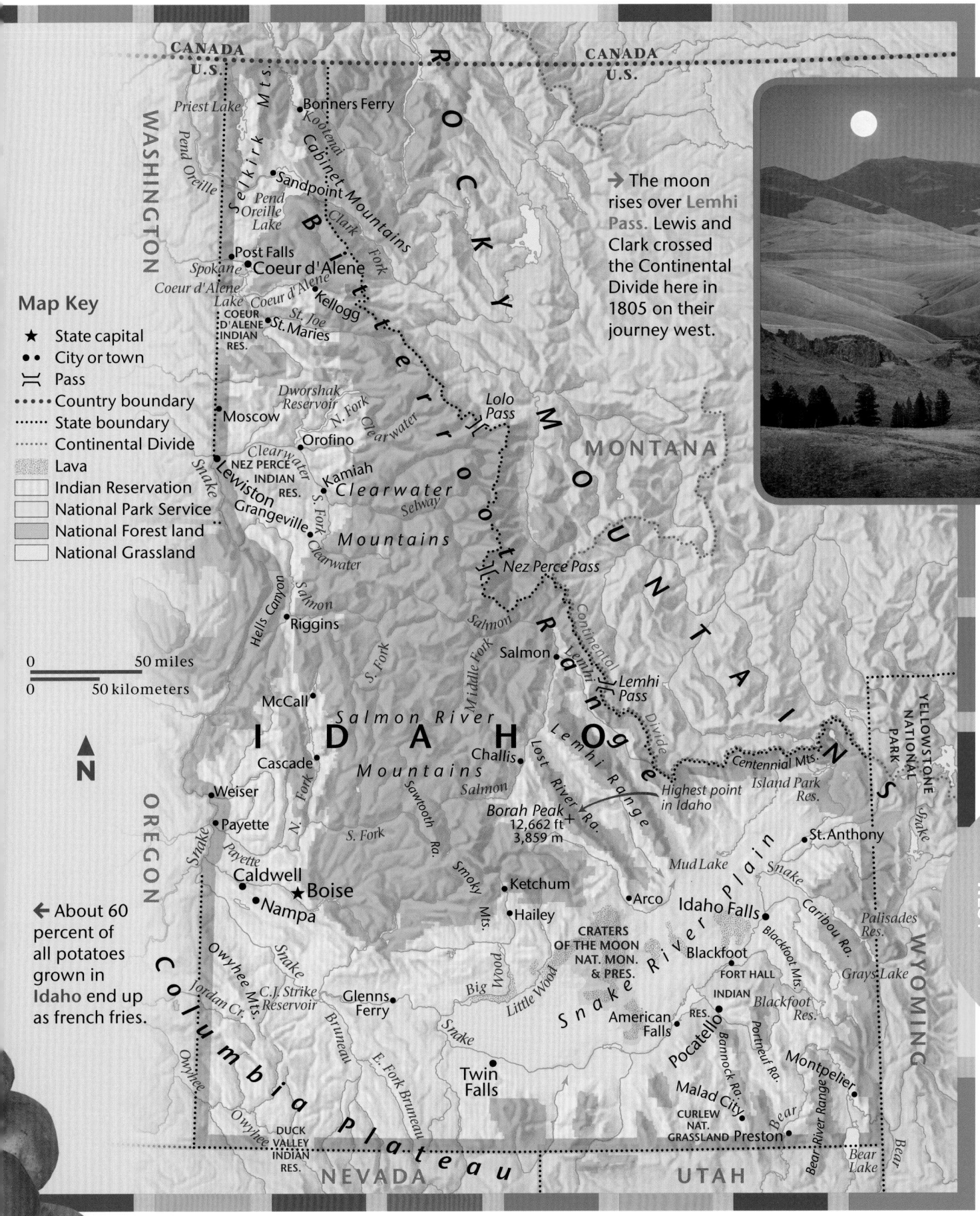

→ The moon rises over **Lemhi Pass.** Lewis and Clark crossed the Continental Divide here in 1805 on their journey west.

← About 60 percent of all potatoes grown in **Idaho** end up as french fries.

Montana

Land & Water The Rocky Mountains, the Great Plains, and the Yellowstone River are important land and water features of Montana.

Statehood Montana became the 41st state in 1889.

People & Places Montana's population is 1,032,949. Helena is the state capital. The largest city is Billings.

Fun Fact Montana is the only state with river systems that empty into the Gulf of Mexico to the southeast, Hudson Bay in Canada, and the Pacific Ocean to the west.

↑ Skiers ride a chairlift up a snowy mountain slope in **Whitefish.**

Montana State Flag

Bitterroot
State Flower

Western Meadowlark
State Bird

↓ Rugged peaks of the northern Rocky Mountains are reflected in the still surface of a mountain lake in **Glacier National Park.**

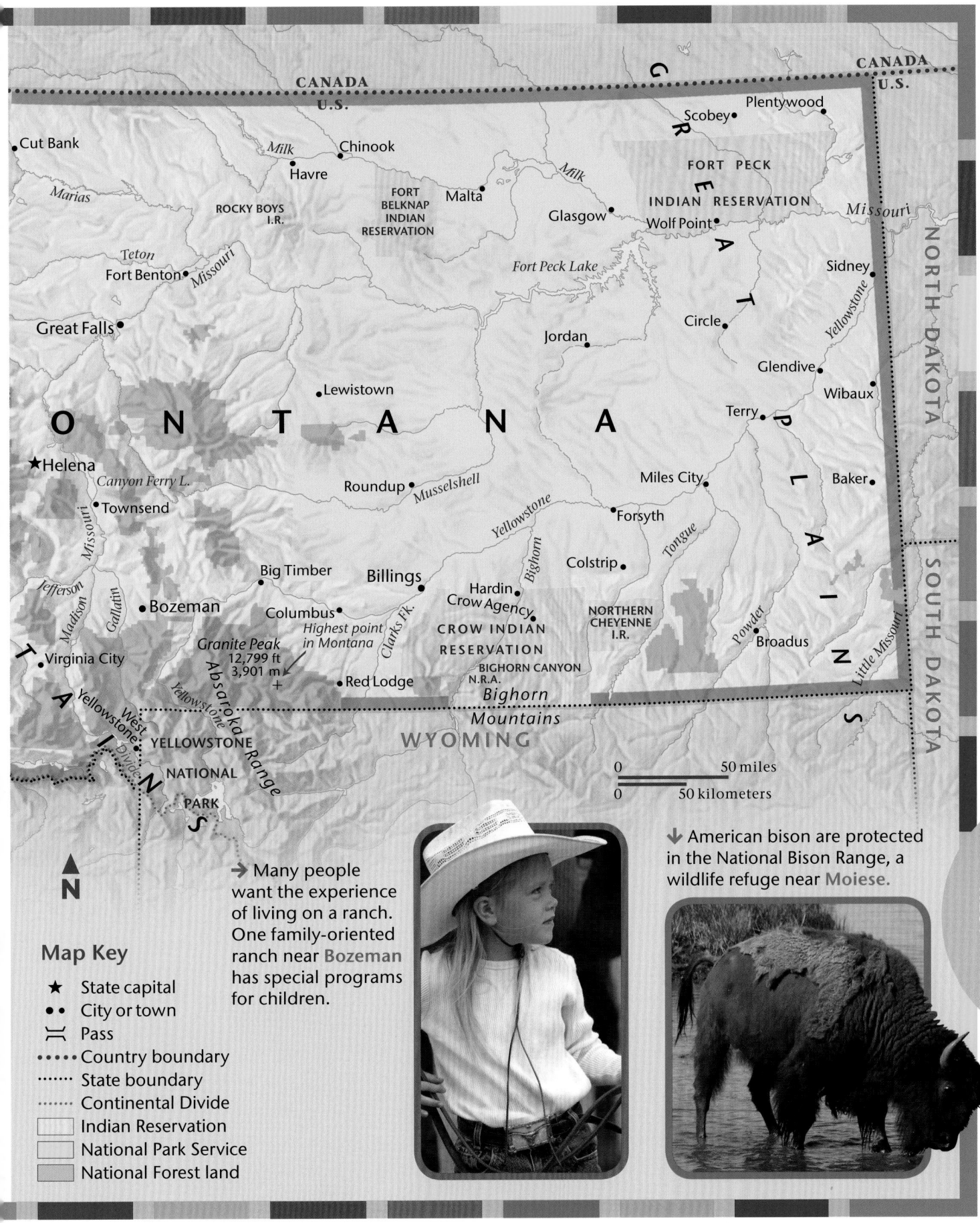

→ Many people want the experience of living on a ranch. One family-oriented ranch near **Bozeman** has special programs for children.

↓ American bison are protected in the National Bison Range, a wildlife refuge near **Moiese**.

Map Key

- ★ State capital
- •• City or town
- Pass
- ••••• Country boundary
- ····· State boundary
- ····· Continental Divide
- Indian Reservation
- National Park Service
- National Forest land

THE WEST

Nevada

Land & Water The Great Basin, the Mojave Desert, and Lake Mead are important land and water features of Nevada.

Statehood Nevada became the 36th state in 1864.

People & Places Nevada's population is 2,890,845. Carson City is the state capital. The largest city is Las Vegas.

Fun Fact Kangaroo rats, which live in the Mojave Desert and other arid areas of the West, are small, seed-eating rodents that can survive with little or no water.

↑ The Luxor, re-creating a scene from ancient Egypt, is one of the many lavish hotels that attract millions of tourists to **Las Vegas.**

← Paiute Indians, dressed in traditional clothing, live on the Pyramid Lake Reservation near **Reno.** Their economy centers on fishing, camping, and other recreational activities.

Nevada State Flag

Mountain Bluebird
State Bird

Sagebrush
State Flower

↓ The desert environment of **Nevada** includes many plants that tolerate very dry conditions. The setting sun highlights mountains in the distance.

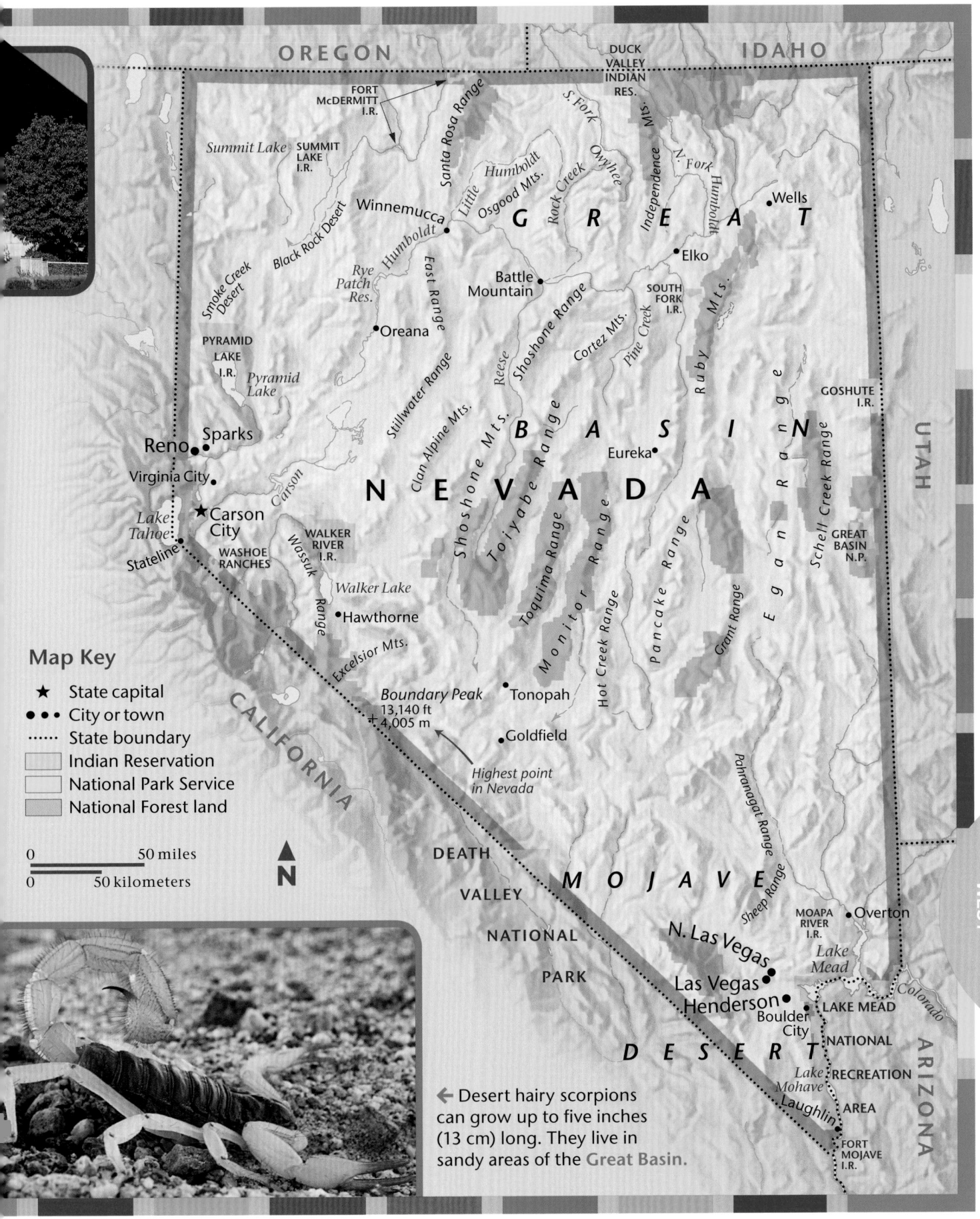

← Desert hairy scorpions can grow up to five inches (13 cm) long. They live in sandy areas of the **Great Basin.**

Oregon

Land & Water The Cascade Range, Crater Lake, and the Columbia River are important land and water features of Oregon.

Statehood Oregon became the 33rd state in 1859.

People & Places Oregon's population is 4,028,977. Salem is the state capital. The largest city is Portland.

Fun Fact The Bonneville Power Administration, headquartered in Portland, provides about 30 percent of the electricity used in the Pacific Northwest. Most of this power comes from hydroelectric plants along the Columbia River.

↑ The 125-foot (38-m) Astoria Column near the mouth of the **Columbia River** is covered with scenes of historic events.

↑ The cool, moist climate of the valley of the **Willamette River** is well suited to certain varieties of wine grapes.

Oregon State Flag

Oregon Grape
State Flower

Western Meadowlark
State Bird

↓ Rocky outcrops called sea stacks line Oregon's **Pacific coast.** They are the remains of a former coastline that has been eroded by waves.

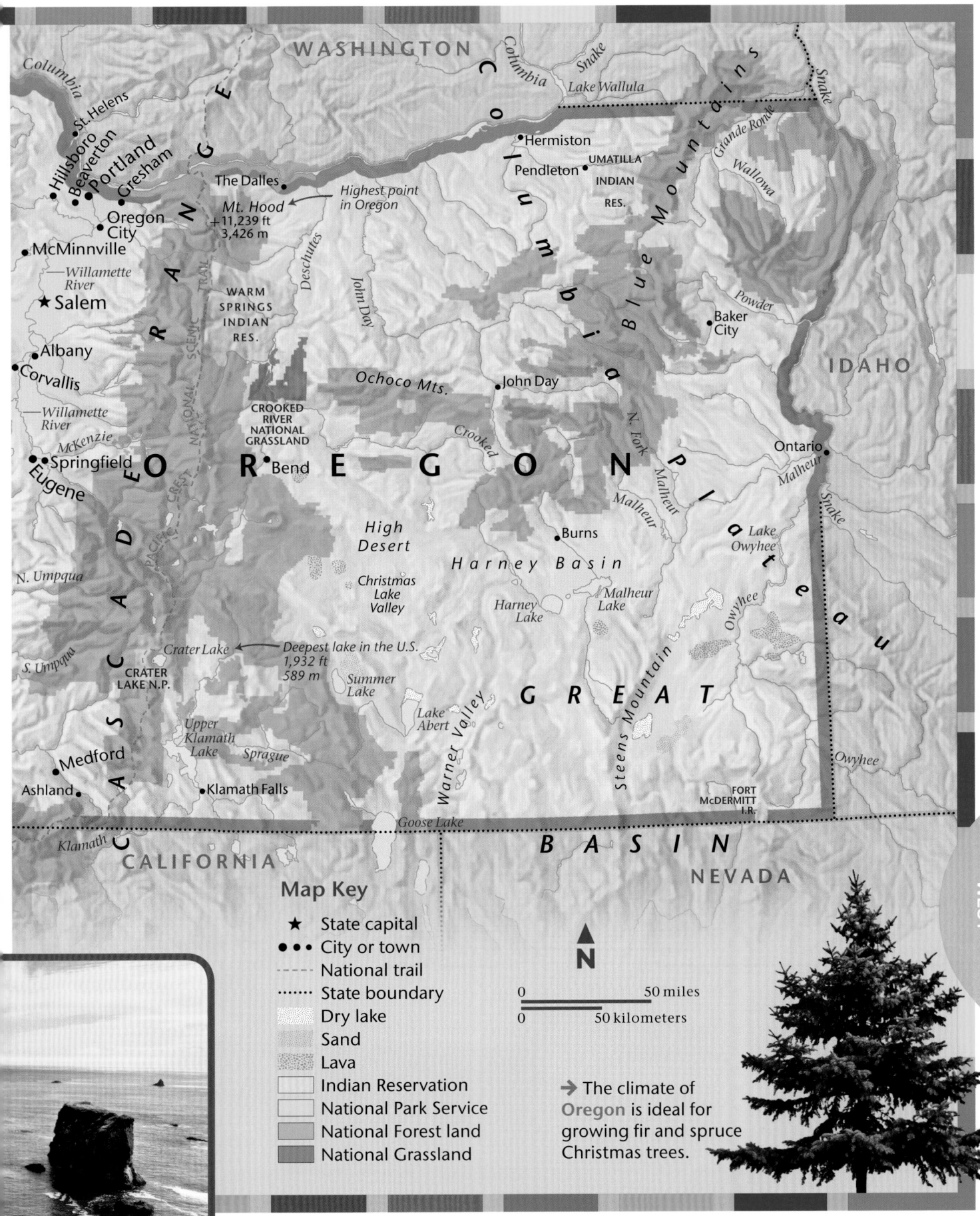

→ The climate of **Oregon** is ideal for growing fir and spruce Christmas trees.

Utah

Land & Water The Great Basin, the Uinta Mountains, and Great Salt Lake are important land and water features of Utah.

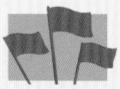

Statehood Utah became the 45th state in 1896.

People & Places Utah's population is 2,995,919. Salt Lake City is the state capital and the largest city.

Fun Fact Great Salt Lake is the largest natural lake west of the Mississippi River. The lake, which has a high level of evaporation, is about eight times saltier than the ocean.

↑ Water sports such as inner tubing are popular activities in **Glen Canyon National Recreation Area.**

← A newly married couple stands in front of the Temple in **Salt Lake City,** where Mormons gather for religious ceremonies.

Utah State Flag

Sego Lilly
State Flower

California Gull
State Bird

↓ Delicate Arch in **Arches National Park** is one of more than 2,000 arches that have been carved by natural forces over millions of years. The snowcapped La Sal Mountains stand in the distance.

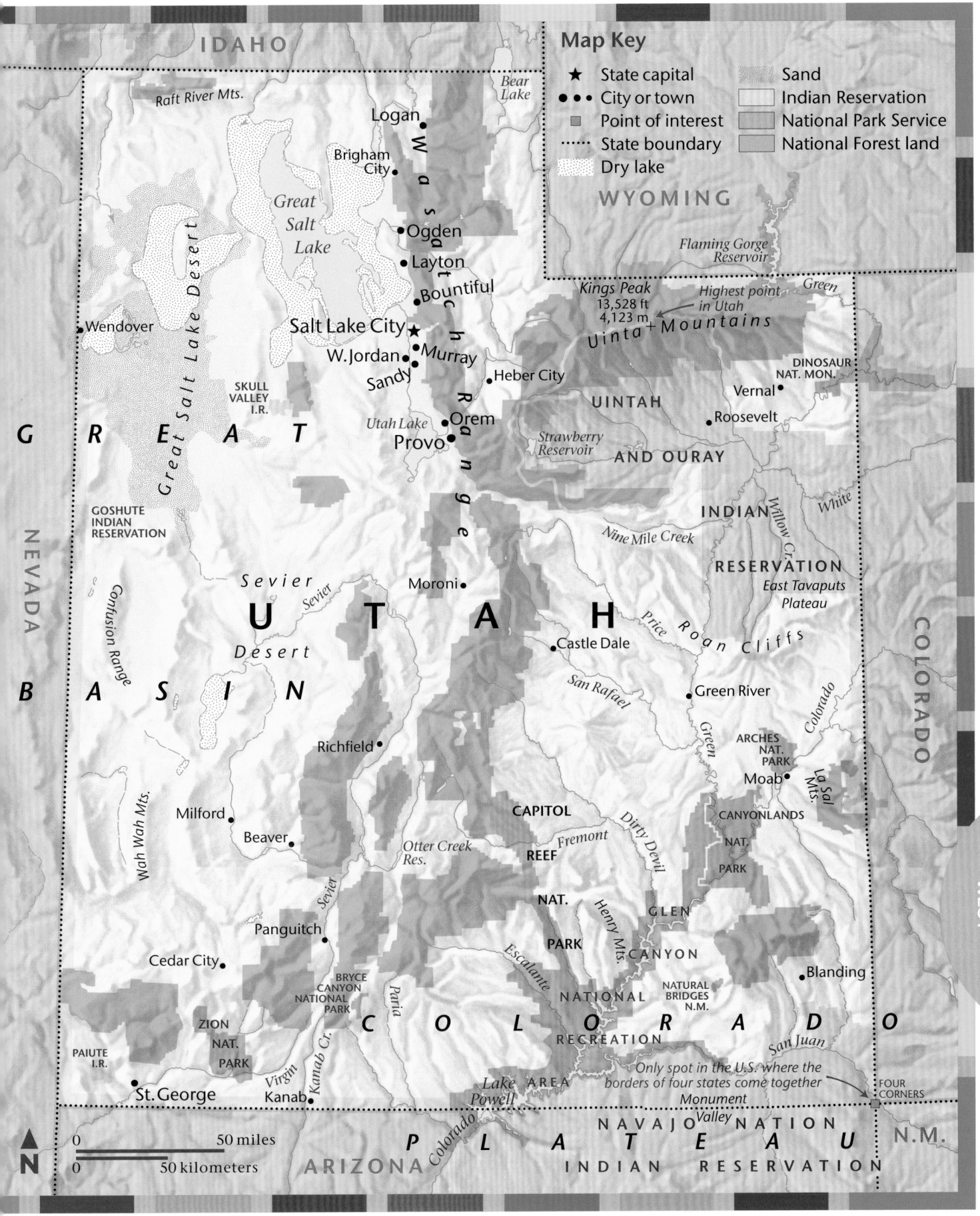
Map Key
State capital
City or town
Point of interest
State boundary
Dry lake
Sand
Indian Reservation
National Park Service
National Forest land
IDAHO
WYOMING
NEVADA
COLORADO
ARIZONA
Raft River Mts.
Bear Lake
Logan
Brigham City
Great Salt Lake
Ogden
Layton
Bountiful
Salt Lake City
Wendover
Great Salt Lake Desert
W. Jordan
Murray
Sandy
Heber City
SKULL VALLEY I.R.
Utah Lake
Orem
Provo
Wasatch Range
Flaming Gorge Reservoir
Kings Peak
13,528 ft
4,123 m
Highest point in Utah
Green
Uinta Mountains
DINOSAUR NAT. MON.
Vernal
UINTAH
Roosevelt
Strawberry Reservoir
AND OURAY
INDIAN
White
Willow Cr.
Nine Mile Creek
RESERVATION
East Tavaputs Plateau
GOSHUTE INDIAN RESERVATION
GREAT
BASIN
Sevier Desert
Sevier
Confusion Range
Moroni
UTAH
Price
Roan Cliffs
Castle Dale
San Rafael
Green River
Colorado
Green
ARCHES NAT. PARK
Moab
La Sal Mts.
Richfield
Wah Wah Mts.
Milford
Beaver
CAPITOL
REEF
NAT.
PARK
Otter Creek Res.
Fremont
Dirty Devil
CANYONLANDS
NAT.
PARK
Sevier
Henry Mts.
GLEN
CANYON
NATIONAL
RECREATION
AREA
Panguitch
Cedar City
Escalante
Blanding
BRYCE CANYON NATIONAL PARK
Paria
NATURAL BRIDGES N.M.
ZION NAT. PARK
PAIUTE I.R.
Virgin
Kanab Cr.
St. George
Kanab
Lake Powell
Only spot in the U.S. where the borders of four states come together
FOUR CORNERS
San Juan
Valley
Colorado
NAVAJO NATION
PLATEAU
INDIAN RESERVATION
N.M.
0 50 miles
0 50 kilometers
N

Washington

Land & Water

The Olympic Mountains, the Palouse Hills, and Puget Sound are important land and water features of Washington.

Statehood

Washington became the 42nd state in 1889.

People & Places

Washington's population is 7,170,351. Olympia is the state capital. The largest city is Seattle.

Fun Fact

Mount Rainier, a dormant volcano, last erupted in 1969. Another nearby volcano, Mount St. Helens, erupted in 1980. Winds carried ash from the eruption as far away as Maine.

↑ A Roosevelt elk grazes in the temperate rain forest of **Olympic National Forest.** Adult males weigh up to 1,000 pounds (454 kg).

Washington State Flag

Coast Rhododendron
State Flower

American Goldfinch
State Bird

← The modern skyline of **Seattle** is easily recognized because of its Space Needle tower. The city is an important West Coast port.

Map Key

- ★ State capital
- ● ● ● City or town
- National trail
- State boundary
- Country boundary
- Glacier
- Indian Reservation
- National Park Service
- National Forest land

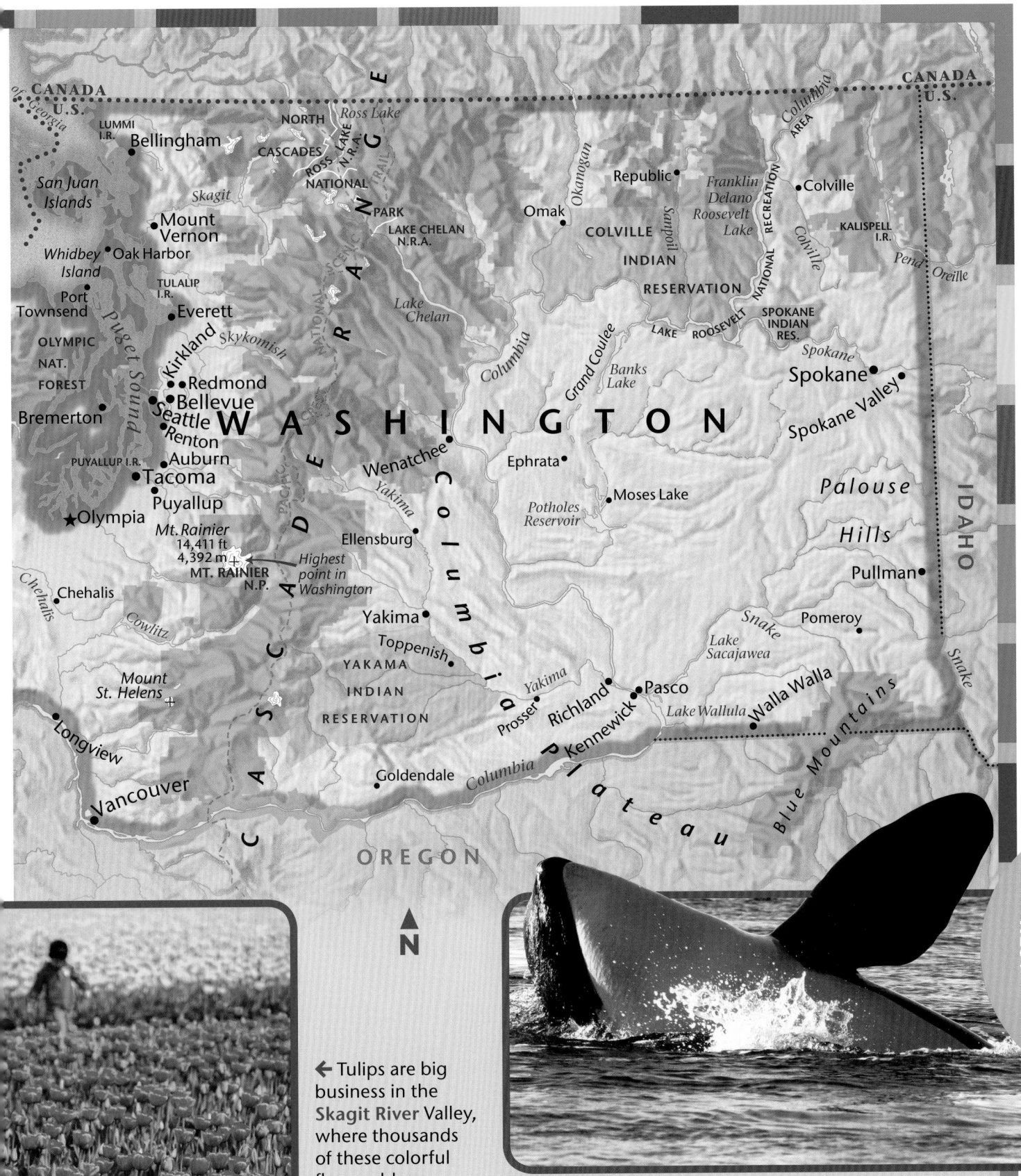

Tulips are big business in the **Skagit River** Valley, where thousands of these colorful flowers bloom every spring.

An orca swims near the **San Juan Islands**. Also known as killer whales, orcas live in groups called pods.

Wyoming

Land & Water

The Rocky Mountains, Yellowstone National Park, and the Green River are important land and water features of Wyoming.

Statehood Wyoming became the 44th state in 1890.

People & Places Wyoming's population is 586,107. Cheyenne is the state capital and the largest city.

Fun Fact Wyoming is called the Equality State because it was the first state to give women the right to vote, granted in 1869 when it was still a territory.

↑ Steam and water from Old Faithful Geyser in Yellowstone National Park erupt more than 100 feet (30 m) into the air.

Map Key

- ★ State capital
- •• City or town
- Pass
- ■ Point of interest
- State Boundary
- Continental Divide
- Indian Reservation
- National Park Service
- National Forest land
- National Grassland

World's first national park, 1872
Yellowstone
Lamar
YELLOWSTONE
Yellowstone Lake
OLD FAITHFUL
NAT. PARK
Continental Divide
JOHN D. ROCKEFELLER, JR. MEM. PKWY.
Snake
Jackson Lake
Teton Range
GRAND TETON NATIONAL PARK
IDAHO
Jackson
Snake
Wyoming Range
Green
Bear
Fontenelle Reservoir
FOSSIL BUTTE NAT. MON.
Hams Fork
Kemmerer
Evanston
Lyman
N
UTAH
0 50 miles
0 50 kilometers

Wyoming State Flag

Indian Paintbrush
State Flower

Western Meadowlark
State Bird

← The Wyoming state capitol building in Cheyenne was completed in 1890. It is now a U.S. national historic landmark.

THE WEST

← The snowcapped peaks of the **Teton Range**, one of the West's youngest ranges, rise high above a meadow where horses graze.

→ Unique to the western **Great Plains**, the pronghorn can sprint up to 60 miles an hour (97 km/h).

The Territories

ACROSS TWO SEAS

Listed below are the five largest* of the fourteen U.S. territories, along with their flags and key information. Two are in the Caribbean Sea; the other three are in the Pacific Ocean. Can you find the other nine U.S. territories on the map?

U.S. CARIBBEAN TERRITORIES

PUERTO RICO

Area: 3,508 sq mi (9,086 sq km)
Population: 3,598,357
Capital: San Juan
Languages: Spanish, English

U.S. VIRGIN ISLANDS

Area: 149 sq mi (386 sq km)
Population: 103,574
Capital: Charlotte Amalie
Languages: English, Spanish or Spanish Creole, French or French Creole

U.S. PACIFIC TERRITORIES

AMERICAN SAMOA

Area: 77 sq mi (199 sq km)
Population: 54,343
Capital: Pago Pago
Languages: Samoan, English

NORTHERN MARIANA ISLANDS

Area: 184 sq mi (477 sq km)
Population: 52,344
Capital: Capital Hill
Languages: Philippine languages, Chamorro, English

GUAM

Area: 217 sq mi (561 sq km)
Population: 161,785
Capital: Hagåtña (Agana)
Languages: English, Filipino, Chamorro

OTHER U.S. TERRITORIES

Baker Island, Howland Island, Jarvis Island, Johnston Atoll, Kingman Reef, Midway Islands, Navassa Island, Palmyra Atoll, Wake Island

*Close-up views of the five largest territories are highlighted in enlarged inset maps labeled with a letter. You can see where each territory is by looking for its corresponding letter on the main map.

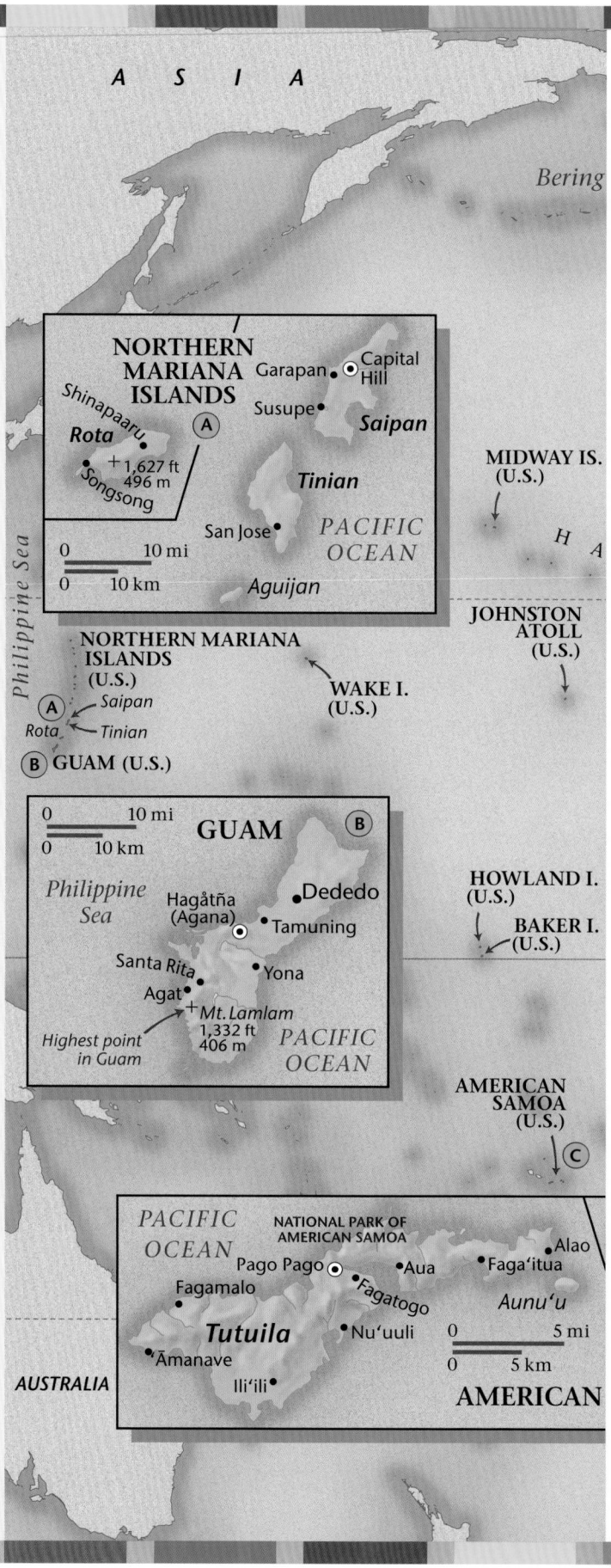

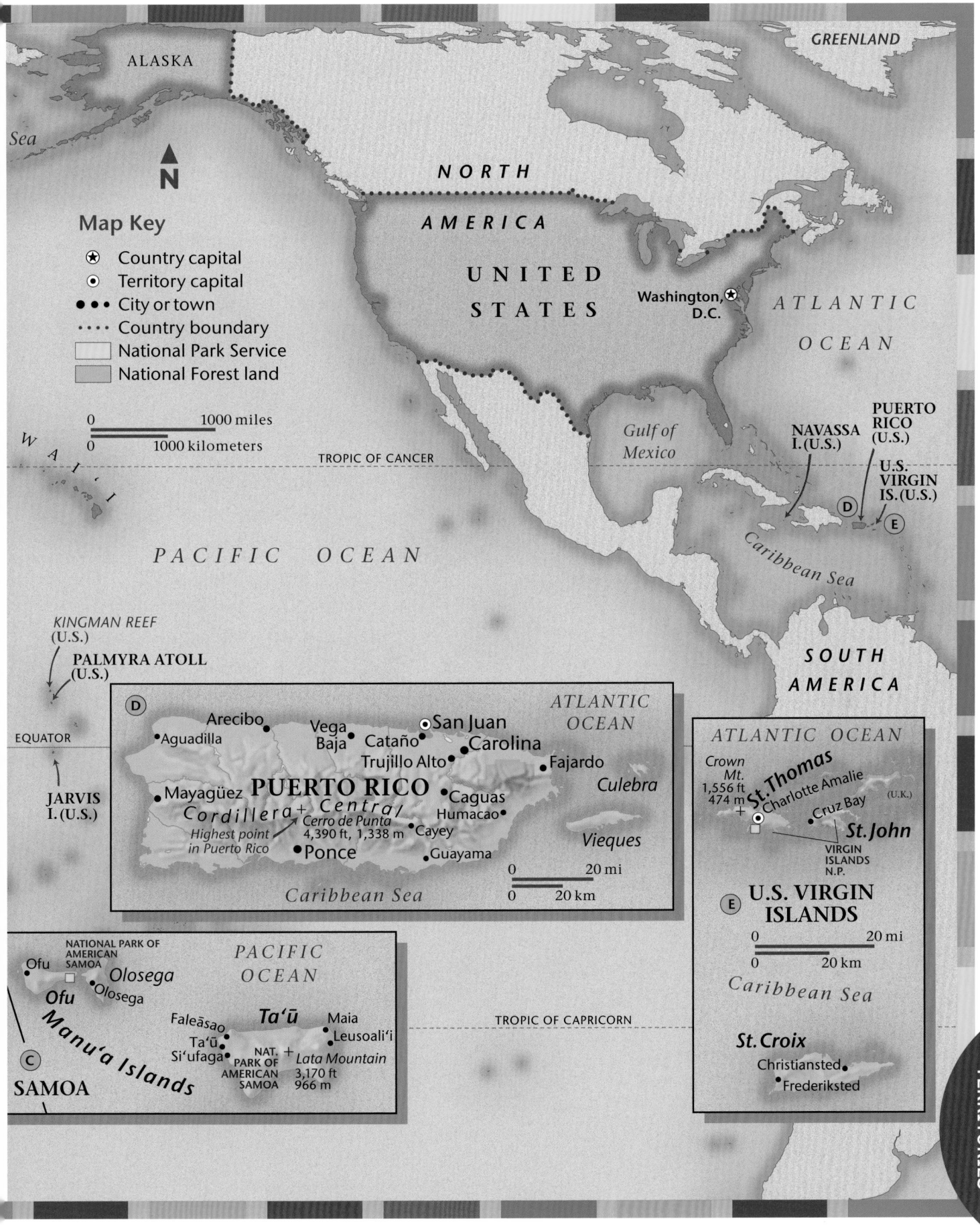
ALASKA
GREENLAND
Sea
N
NORTH
AMERICA
Map Key
Country capital
Territory capital
City or town
Country boundary
National Park Service
National Forest land
UNITED
STATES
Washington, D.C.
ATLANTIC
OCEAN
0 1000 miles
0 1000 kilometers
W A I I I
TROPIC OF CANCER
Gulf of Mexico
NAVASSA I. (U.S.)
PUERTO RICO (U.S.)
U.S. VIRGIN IS. (U.S.)
D
E
PACIFIC OCEAN
Caribbean Sea
KINGMAN REEF (U.S.)
PALMYRA ATOLL (U.S.)
SOUTH
AMERICA
EQUATOR
JARVIS I. (U.S.)
D
ATLANTIC OCEAN
Arecibo
Aguadilla
Vega Baja
San Juan
Cataño
Carolina
Trujillo Alto
Fajardo
Culebra
Mayagüez
PUERTO RICO
Caguas
Cordillera Central
Cerro de Punta 4,390 ft, 1,338 m
Humacao
Highest point in Puerto Rico
Cayey
Ponce
Guayama
Vieques
0 20 mi
0 20 km
Caribbean Sea
ATLANTIC OCEAN
Crown Mt. 1,556 ft 474 m
St. Thomas
Charlotte Amalie
Cruz Bay
(U.K.)
St. John
VIRGIN ISLANDS N.P.
E
U.S. VIRGIN ISLANDS
0 20 mi
0 20 km
Caribbean Sea
St. Croix
Christiansted
Frederiksted
NATIONAL PARK OF AMERICAN SAMOA
Ofu
Olosega
Ofu
Olosega
PACIFIC OCEAN
Manu'a Islands
Faleāsao
Ta'ū
Maia
Leusoali'i
Ta'ū
Si'ufaga
NAT. PARK OF AMERICAN SAMOA
Lata Mountain 3,170 ft 966 m
C
SAMOA
TROPIC OF CAPRICORN

The United States at a Glance

Land

Five Largest States by Area

1. **Alaska:** 663,267 sq mi (1,717,854 sq km)
2. **Texas:** 268,581 sq mi (695,624 sq km)
3. **California:** 163,696 sq mi (423,972 sq km)
4. **Montana:** 147,042 sq mi (380,840 sq km)
5. **New Mexico:** 121,590 sq mi (314,917 sq km)

Water

Primary Water Bodies Bordering the U.S.

1. **Pacific Ocean:** 65,436,200 sq mi (169,479,000 sq km)
2. **Atlantic Ocean:** 35,338,500 sq mi (91,526,400 sq km)
3. **Arctic Ocean:** 5,390,000 sq mi (13,960,100 sq km)
4. **Gulf of Mexico:** 591,430 sq mi (1,531,810 sq km)

Highest, Longest, Largest

The numbers below show locations on the map.

❶ **Highest Mountain**
Denali (Mount McKinley), in Alaska:
20,320 ft (6,194 m)

❷ **Longest River System**
Mississippi–Missouri: 3,710 mi (5,971 km)

❸ **Largest Freshwater Lake (entirely in the U.S.)**
Lake Michigan:
22,300 sq mi (57,757 sq km)

❹ **Largest Saltwater Lake**
Great Salt Lake, in Utah:
1,700 sq mi (4,403 sq km)

❺ **Northernmost Point**
Point Barrow, Alaska

❻ **Southernmost Point**
Kalae, Hawai'i

❼ **Easternmost Point**
Sail Rock, West Quoddy Head, Maine

❽ **Westernmost Point**
Peaked Island, Alaska

People

In 2015 more than 320 million people live in the United States. Of these, more than 43 million were born in another country. The largest foreign-born group came from Mexico, followed by India, the Philippines, and China. By 2050 it is estimated that the country's population will approach 400 million, with 72 million being foreign-born.

Five Largest States by Number of People

1. **California:** 39,144,818 people
2. **Texas:** 27,469,114 people
3. **Florida:** 20,271,272 people
4. **New York:** 19,795,791 people
5. **Illinois:** 12,859,995 people

Five Largest Cities* by Number of People

1. **New York, NY:** 8,491,079 people
2. **Los Angeles, CA:** 3,928,864 people
3. **Chicago, IL:** 2,722,389 people
4. **Houston, TX:** 2,239,558 people
5. **Philadelphia, PA:** 1,560,297 people

*Figures are for city proper, not metropolitan area.

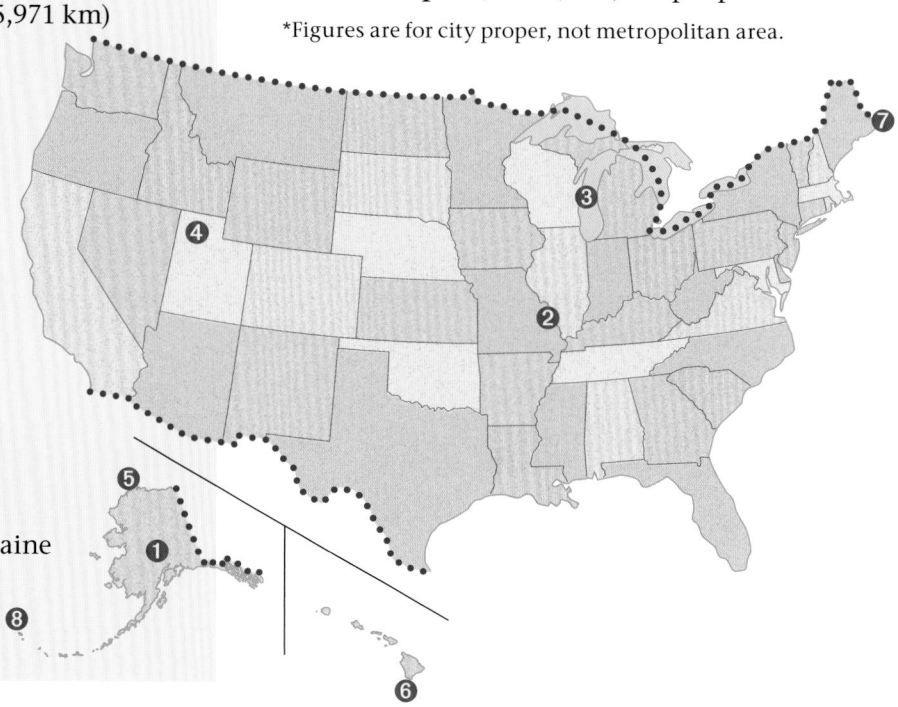

Glossary

Barrier island: a long sandy island that runs parallel to a shore

Bicentennial: the 200th anniversary of an event

Border State: during the Civil War, a slave state that stayed in the Union (Delaware, Kentucky, Maryland, and Missouri)

Boundary: an imaginary line that separates one political or mapped area from another; physical features (such as mountains and rivers) or latitude and longitude lines sometimes act as boundaries

Capital: a place where a country or state government is located

Coniferous forest: needleleaf trees that bear seeds in cones

Container ships: large ships that carry goods in truck-size metal containers among world ports

Contiguous U.S.: the 48 states that are joined together; excludes Alaska and Hawai'i

Continental U.S.: the 49 states located on the continent of North America; excludes Hawai'i

Continental Divide: a natural boundary line separating waters flowing into the Atlantic Ocean and Gulf of Mexico from those flowing into the Pacific Ocean

Creole: a blended language evolved from contact between two or more unrelated languages

Deciduous forests: trees, such as oak, maple, and beech, that lose their leaves in the cold season

Delmarva Peninsula: an East Coast peninsula named for the states it includes: Delaware, Maryland, and Virginia

Desert: a region with either hot or cold temperatures that receives ten inches (25 cm) or less of precipitation a year

Dormant volcano: a volcano that is currently inactive but that may erupt at some time in the future

Erosion: the process by which wind, water, or ice carries away rocks, soil, and other weathered material on Earth's surface

Estuary: the wide part of a river near a sea, where freshwater and saltwater mix

Exports: products made in one place and sent to another to be sold

Foothills: a region of lower hills at the base of a mountain

Fossil: an impression left by the remains of ancient animals or plants that has been preserved in rock or tree sap

Grassland: large areas of mainly flat land covered with grasses

High Plains: flat or gently rolling land above 2,000 feet (600 m); semiarid region east of the Rocky Mountains

Hydroelectric plant: a facility that uses the energy of moving water to create power

Indian reservation: land set aside by the U.S. government for Native Americans to live on and govern

Louisiana Purchase: land purchased from France in 1803 that stretched from the Mississippi River to the Rocky Mountains, and from the Gulf of Mexico to Canada, doubling the size of the country at that time

Mouth: place where a river empties into an ocean or other large body of water

Peninsula: a large piece of land that sticks out into the water

Petroleum: a type of fuel formed when the remains of marine plants and animals are buried beneath sediments and subjected to intense heat and pressure over millions of years

Sedimentary: a kind of rock, such as sandstone, made of small, compressed particles

Shakers: members of a religious group who did not marry and lived in communal societies

Sunbelt: a region of the southern and western U.S. experiencing rapid economic growth and major in-migration of population

Territory: land under the rule of a country but that is not a state or a province of that country

Temperate rain forest: forests found along the Pacific coast of North America where there is a cool, moist climate and where rainfall is abundant

Tropical rain forest: a region occurring mostly in a belt between the Tropic of Cancer and Tropic of Capricorn in areas that have at least 80 inches (200 cm) of rain each year and an average yearly temperature of 77°F (25°C)

Tundra: a region at high latitudes or high elevations that has cold temperatures, low vegetation, and a short growing season

Wetland: land that is covered with or soaked by water; includes swamps, marshes, and bogs

Index

Pictures and the text that describes them have their page numbers printed in **bold** type.

A

Airplanes **53**
Alabama 38–39
Alaska **6,** 100–101
Alligators **44**
American Samoa 122–123
Amish **83**
Arizona 90–91
Arkansas 40–41
Atlanta, Georgia **44**

B

Bald eagles **6, 86**
Baseball **8, 22, 64**
Basketball 22, **52**
Beaches **6, 16–17, 38, 50, 102**
Bison **80, 111**
Black bears **12, 25**
Bridges **20, 38–39, 50, 61, 72, 96, 102**

C

California 102–103
Catfish **50**
Caves **59, 92**
Chesapeake Bay **20, 21**
Coal mining **60**
Colorado **7, 98–99,** 104–105
Connecticut 14–15
Corn **66–67**
Crabs **21, 101**
Cranberries **22**

D

Dams **56,** 114
Deer **57, 77**
Delaware 16–17
Deserts **6, 90, 112, 113**
Dinosaurs 84, **84**
District of Columbia 10–11
Dog sledding **100**

E

Earthquakes 100

F

Farms **27, 35, 40, 51, 62–63, 66–67, 68, 86**
Fishing **41, 74**
Florida **36,** 42–43
Forests **6, 60, 108**
Fossils **80**

G

Georgia **36–37,** 44–45
Guam 122

H

Hawai'i **6,** 106–107
Herons **59**
Horses **21, 47, 88, 121**
Hot-air balloons **92**

I

Idaho 108–109
Illinois **9,** 64–65
Indian mounds 58, **69**
Indian powwows and festivals **68, 75, 86, 90**
Indian reservations **85,** 90, **112**
Indiana 66–67
Indians of North America 68, **78–79,** 94, **95, 100, 104**
Iowa 68–69

K

Kansas **62–63,** 70–71
Kentucky 46–47

L

Lewis and Clark Expedition **76, 109**
Lighthouses **17, 18–19, 32, 53**
Lincoln, Abraham **10, 46, 65, 84**
Louisiana 48–49

M

Maine 18–19
Manatees **42**
Maple trees **34**
Mardi Gras **48, 49**
Maryland 20–21
Massachusetts 22–23
Michigan 72–73
Minnesota 74–75
Mississippi 50–51
Mississippi River **48, 50,** 76
Missouri 76–77
Monopoly 26, **26**
Montana 110–111
Moose **18**
Mormons **116**
Music **48, 57, 58,** 72, **82**

N

Nebraska 78–79
Nevada 112–113
New Hampshire 24–25

Two-Letter Postal Codes

New Jersey 26–27
New Mexico 92–93
New York **12–13,** 28–29
New York, New York **9, 26, 28–29**
Niagara Falls **12–13**
North Carolina 52–53
North Dakota 80–81
Northern Mariana Islands 122

O

Ohio 82–83
Oil industry **94, 96**
Oklahoma 94–95
Oregon 114–115

P

Peaches **45**
Peanuts **44**
Pennsylvania 30–31
Pigs **64, 68**
Pioneers **71, 78–79**
Potatoes 24, **108–109**
Prairie dogs **78**
Pronghorn **121**
Puerto Rico 122, 123
Pumpkins **9,** 16

R

Rhode Island 32–33
Rice **40**
Rodeos **80**
Roller coasters **26, 82**
Roosevelt, Theodore **81, 84**

S

Sailing **20, 32-33, 86**
Ships **14, 23, 38, 54**
Shrimp **48**
South Carolina 54–55
South Dakota 84–85
Space program **42,** 108
Statue of Liberty **29**
Surfboarding **106–107**

T

Tennessee 56–57
Territories 122–123
Texas **88–89,** 96–97
Tornadoes **94**
Turtles **55, 107**

U

U.S. Virgin Islands 122, 123
Utah **6,** 116–117

V

Vermont 34–35
Virginia 58–59
Volcanoes 106, **106,** 118

W

Washington 118–119
Washington, D.C. 10–11
West Virginia 60–61
Whales 14, **23, 119**
Whitewater rafting **60–61, 90**
Winter sports **24, 32, 35, 86, 105, 110**
Wisconsin 86–87
Wolves **74**
Wyoming 120–121

Two-Letter Postal Codes

ALABAMA	AL
ALASKA	AK
ARIZONA	AZ
ARKANSAS	AR
CALIFORNIA	CA
COLORADO	CO
CONNECTICUT	CT
DELAWARE	DE
DISTRICT OF COLUMBIA	DC
FLORIDA	FL
GEORGIA	GA
HAWAI'I	HI
IDAHO	ID
ILLINOIS	IL
INDIANA	IN
IOWA	IA
KANSAS	KS
KENTUCKY	KY
LOUISIANA	LA
MAINE	ME
MARYLAND	MD
MASSACHUSETTS	MA
MICHIGAN	MI
MINNESOTA	MN
MISSISSIPPI	MS
MISSOURI	MO
MONTANA	MT
NEBRASKA	NE
NEVADA	NV
NEW HAMPSHIRE	NH
NEW JERSEY	NJ
NEW MEXICO	NM
NEW YORK	NY
NORTH CAROLINA	NC
NORTH DAKOTA	ND
OHIO	OH
OKLAHOMA	OK
OREGON	OR
PENNSYLVANIA	PA
PUERTO RICO	PR
RHODE ISLAND	RI
SOUTH CAROLINA	SC
SOUTH DAKOTA	SD
TENNESSEE	TN
TEXAS	TX
UTAH	UT
VERMONT	VT
VIRGINIA	VA
WASHINGTON	WA
WEST VIRGINIA	WV
WISCONSIN	WI
WYOMING	WY

Copyright © 2016 National Geographic Partners, LLC

All rights reserved. Reproduction of the whole or any part of the contents without written permission from the publisher is prohibited.

Since 1888, the National Geographic Society has funded more than 12,000 research, exploration, and preservation projects around the world. The Society receives funds from National Geographic Partners, LLC, funded in part by your purchase. A portion of the proceeds from this book supports this vital work. To learn more, visit www.natgeo.com/info.

For more information, visit www.nationalgeographic.com, call 1-800-647-5463, or write to the following address:
National Geographic Partners, LLC
1145 17th Street N.W.
Washington, D.C. 20036-4688 U.S.A.

Visit us online at nationalgeographic.com/books

For librarians and teachers: ngchildrensbooks.org

More for kids from National Geographic: kids.nationalgeographic.com

For information about special discounts for bulk purchases, please contact National Geographic Books Special Sales: ngspecsales@ngs.org

For rights or permissions inquiries, please contact National Geographic Books Subsidiary Rights: ngbookrights@ngs.org

NATIONAL GEOGRAPHIC and Yellow Border Design are trademarks of the National Geographic Society, used under license.

Designed by Jim Hiscott, Jr.

Paperback ISBN: 978-1-4263-2647-9
Hardcover ISBN: 978-1-4263-2434-5
Reinforced library binding ISBN: 978-1-4263-2435-2

Printed in China
16/RRDS/1

Illustrations Credits

Front cover: (background), Brandon Laufenberg/Getty Images; (Sacagawea), Patrick Faricy; (George Washington), Everett Historical/Shutterstock; (boy on rope swing), Corbis; (U.S. globe), ymgerman/iStockphoto; (baseball), Dan Thornberg/Shutterstock; (Seattle Space Needle), Digital Stock; (Route 66 sign), Photodisc; (Lincoln Memorial), Alexander Shor/E+/Getty Images; (cherry pie), BRAND X; (bald eagle), EyeWire Images; (totem pole), Photodisc; (stamp outline), Neftali/Shutterstock; (stamp outline), stamp outline/Shutterstock; **Spine:** (Chrysler Building), Danita Delimont/Getty Images; **Back cover:** (riverboat), Photodisc; (lizard), MWaits/Shutterstock; (lake and mountain), Photodisc; (bald eagle flying), Sekar B/Shutterstock; (hot dog), mj007/Shutterstock

Front matter: 1 (background), Brandon Laufenberg/Getty Images; 1 (UP LE), zschnepf/Shutterstock; 1 (UP RT), Taylor Kennedy/National Geographic Creative; 1 (LO LE), Eric Isselée/Shutterstock; 1 (LO RT), John Kelly/Iconica/Getty Images; 1 (LO CTR), Paul Tillinghast/Getty Images; 2 (LE), Alaska Stock Images/NationalGeographicStock.com; 2 (RT), SergeyIT/Shutterstock; 2 (LO), Rob Byron/Shutterstock; 3 (UP LE), metalstock/Shutterstock; 3 (LO LE), Zuzule/Shutterstock; 3 (UP RT), Eric Isselée/Shutterstock; 3 (CTR), James M Phelps, Jr/Shutterstock; 3 (RT), Geoffrey Kuchera/Shutterstock; 6 (LO LE), erllre74/Shutterstock; 6 (UP RT), Charles Krebs/Riser/Getty Images; 6 (CTR RT), Mike Brake/Shutterstock; 6 (LO RT), James Randklev/Riser/Getty Images; 7, Olivier Le Queinec/Shutterstock; 8 (UP), Billy Hustace/Stone/Getty Images; 8 (LO), sonya etchison/Shutterstock; 9 (LE), Mark R/Shutterstock; 9 (RT), dibrova/Shutterstock; 10 (CTR), PhotoDisc; 10-11 (UP), PhotoDisc; 11 (UP RT), Taylor S. Kennedy/NationalGeographicStock.com; 11 (LO), Jahi Chikwendiu/The Washington Post/Getty Images; **THE NORTHEAST:** 12 (LO), Alaska Stock Images/NationalGeographicStock.com; 12-13, Skip Brown/NationalGeographicStock.com; 14 (UP), Shawn Pecor/Shutterstock; 14 (LO), Donald Gargano/Shutterstock; 15, Joel Sartore/NationalGeographicStock.com; 16 (CTR), Kevin Fleming/Corbis; 16-17 (UP), Jake Rajs/Stome/Getty Images; 16-17 (LO), William S. Kuta/Alamy/Alamy; 17 (UP RT), Catherine Lane/iStockphoto.com; 18 (CTR), Mikael Damkier/Shutterstock; 18 (LO), Jeff Schultes/Shutterstock; 18-19 (UP), PhotoDisc; 19 (LO), Noah Strycker/Shutterstock; 20 (UP), Emory Kristof/NationalGeographicStock.com; 20 (LO), Jeremy Edwards/iStockphoto.com; 21 (UP), Justine Gecewicz/iStockphoto.com; 21 (LO), James L. Stanfield/NationalGeographicStock.com; 22 (UP), Christopher Penler/Shutterstock; 22 (LO), Lijuan Guo/Shutterstock; 23 (LE), Chee-Onn Leong/Shutterstock; 23 (RT), Brett Atkins/Shutterstock; 24 (UP), Paula Stephens/Shutterstock; 24 (CTR), Marcel Jancovic/Shutterstock; 24 (LO), George & Judy Manna/Photo Researchers RM/Getty Images; 25, Tony Campbell/Shutterstock; 26 (UP), Dave Raboin/iStockphoto.com; 26 (CTR), Steve Miller/The Star-Ledger/Corbis; 26-27 (LO), Aimin Tang/iStockphoto.com; 27 (UP), Sheldon Kralstein/iStockphoto.com; 27 (CTR), Andrew F. Kazmierski/Shutterstock; 28 (UP), Cathleen Abers-Kimball/iStockphoto.com; 28-29 (LO), Richard Levine/Alamy; 29 (RT), Glenn Taylor/iStockphoto.com; 30, iStockphoto.com; 31 (LE), Jeremy Edwards/iStockphoto.com; 31 (RT), Racheal Grazias/Shutterstock; 32 (CTR), Mona Makela/Shutterstock; 32 (LO), Joy Brown/Shutterstock; 32-33 (UP), Yare Marketing/Shutterstock; 33 (LO), Robert Kelsey/Shutterstock; 34 (UP), Thomas M Perkins/Shutterstock; 34 (LO), sianc/Shutterstock; 35 (UP), Parker Deen/iStockphoto.com; 35 (LO), rebvt/Shutterstock; **THE SOUTHEAST:** 36 (LO), SergeyIT/Shutterstock; 36-37, Maria Stenzel/NationalGeographicStock.com; 38 (UP), Darryl Vest/Shutterstock; 38 (CTR), Kevin Fleming/Corbis; 38-39 (LO), Wayne James/Shutterstock; 39 (CTR), Ronnie Howard/Shutterstock; 40 (UP), courtesy of the Museum of Discovery, www.museumofdiscovery.org; 40 (LO), Bill Barksdale/Corbis; 41, Travel Bug/Shutterstock; 42 (UP), Wayne Johnson/iStockphoto.com; 42 (LO), NASA; 43 (UP), Varina and Jay Patel/iStockphoto.com; 43 (LO), Valentyn Volkov/Shutterstock; 44 (UP), jackweichen_gatech/Shutterstock; 44 (CTR), Antonio V. Oquias/Shutterstock; 44 (LO), Brian Lasenby/Shutterstock; 45, Andrew F. Kazmierski/Shutterstock; 46 (UP), Leon Ritter/Shutterstock; 46 (CTR), Craig Wactor/Shutterstock; 46 (LO), Anne Kitzman/Shutterstock; 47, Neale Cousland/Shutterstock; 48 (UP), Bob Sacha/Corbis; 48 (CTR), Jim Richardson/Corbis; 48 (LO), J. Helgason/Shutterstock; 49 (LE), Stephen Helstowski/Shutterstock; 49 (RT), Kathryn Bell/Shutterstock; 50 (UP), Vilmos Varga/Shutterstock; 50 (CTR), Daniela Duncan/Getty Images; 50 (LO), Peter Arnold, Inc./Alamy; 51, Mike Flippo/Shutterstock; 52 (LE), Leah-Anne Thompson/Shutterstock; 52 (RT), Forrest L. Smith, III/Shutterstock; 53 (LE), Rob Byron/Shutterstock; 53 (RT), Brad Whitsitt/Shutterstock; 54, Rafael Ramirez Lee/Shutterstock; 55 (UP), Richard Ellis/Getty Images; 55 (LO), Zach Holmes/Alamy; 56 (UP), Envision/Corbis; 56 (LO), Bryan Busovicki/Shutterstock; 57 (LE), Wayne James/Shutterstock; 57 (RT), Jennifer King/Shutterstock; 58 (UP), Darren K. Fisher/Shutterstock; 58 (LO), Travel Bug/Shutterstock; 59 (LE), graham s. klotz/Shutterstock; 59 (RT), Adam Bies/Shutterstock; 60 (CTR), Ken Inness/Shutterstock; 60 (LO), Mary Terriberry/Shutterstock; 60-61 (UP), Robert Pernell/Shutterstock; 61 (RT), Adam Bies/Shutterstock; **THE MIDWEST:** 62 (LO), metalstock/Shutterstock; 62-63, Jim Brandenburg/Minden Pictures; 64 (UP), Ralf-Finn Hestoft/Corbis; 64 (CTR), Tim Boyle/Getty Images; 64 (LO), Jenny Solomon/Shutterstock; 65, Kim Karpeles/Alamy; 66 (UP), James Steidl/Shutterstock; 66 (UP), Todd Taulman/Shutterstock; 66 (CTR), john j. klaiber jr/Shutterstock; 66-67 (LO), Melissa Farlow/NationalGeographicStock.com; 68 (UP), jokter/Shutterstock; 68 (LO), Madeleine Openshaw/Shutterstock; 69 (LE), steve schneider/iStockphoto.com; 69 (RT), Andre Jenny/Alamy; 70 (UP), aceshot1/Shutterstock; 70 (LO), Rusty Dodson/Shutterstock; 71, Bruce Dale/NationalGeographicStock.com; 72 (UP), Gary Paul Lewis/Shutterstock; 72 (CTR), Rachel L. Sellers/Shutterstock; 72 (LO), John Brueske/Shutterstock; 73, Cornelia Schaible/iStockphoto.com; 74 (UP), Maxim Kulko/Shutterstock; 74 (CTR), V. J. Matthew/Shutterstock; 74 (LO), Geoffrey Kuchera/Shutterstock; 75, Karla Caspari/Shutterstock; 76 (UP), Neil Phillip Mey/Shutterstock; 76 (LO), Jose Gil/Shutterstock; 77 (LE), Tim Pleasant/Shutterstock; 77 (RT), Rusty Dodson/Shutterstock; 78 (UP), Bates Littlehales/NationalGeographicStock.com; 78-79 (LO), James L. Amos/NationalGeographicStock.com; 79 (UP), Joel Sartore/NationalGeographicStock.com; 79 (LO RT), Jim Richardson/NationalGeographicStock.com; 80 (UP), Ian Martin/NationalGeographicStock.com; 80 (CTR), Randy Olson/NationalGeographicStock.com; 80 (LO), Rusty Dodson/Shutterstock; 81, iofoto/Shutterstock; 82 (UP), aceshot1/Shutterstock; 82 (CTR), Alex Neauville/Shutterstock; 82 (LO), James M Phelps, Jr/Shutterstock; 83, Weldon Schloneger/Shutterstock; 84 (UP), Werner Bollmann/Photolibrary/Getty Images; 84 (CTR), Ira Block/NationalGeographicStock.com; 84 (LO), iofoto/Shutterstock; 85, Danita Delimont/Alamy; 86 (UP LE), Aga/Shutterstock; 86 (UP RT), Brad Thompson/Shutterstock; 86 (CTR), Volkman K. Wentzel/NationalGeographicStock.com; 86 (LO), Alvis Upitis/AgStock Images/Corbis; 87, Layne Kennedy/Corbis; **THE SOUTHWEST:** 88 (LO), Zuzule/Shutterstock; 88-89, Jack Dykinga/NationalGeographicStock.com; 90 (UP), Michael Nichols/NationalGeographicStock.com; 90 (CTR), Zschnepf/Shutterstock; 90 (LO), Chris Curtis/Shutterstock; 92 (UP), italianestro/Shutterstock; 92 (CTR), Mariusz S. Jurgielewicz/Shutterstock; 92 (LO), Ralph Lee Hopkins/NationalGeographicStock.com; 94 (UP), Clint Spencer/iStockphoto.com; 94 (LO), Phil Anthony/Shutterstock; 95 (LE), Lindsay Hebberd/Corbis; 95 (RT), MWaits/Shutterstock; 96 (UP), Ben Conlan/iStockphoto.com; 96 (CTR), Mira/Alamy; 96 (LO), Rusty Dodson/Shutterstock; 97, B. Anthony Stewart/NationalGeographicStock.com; **THE WEST:** 98 (LO), Eric Isselée/Shutterstock; 98-99, Gordon Wiltsie/NationalGeographicStock.com; 100 (UP), Benoit Rousseau/iStockphoto.com; 100 (LO), alysta/Shutterstock; 101, Michael Pemberton/Shutterstock; 102 (UP), Stas Volik/Shutterstock; 102 (CTR), Bates Littlehales/NationalGeographicStock.com; 102 (LO), Lindsay Noechel/Shutterstock; 103, Elke Dennis/Shutterstock; 104 (UP), Larsek/Shutterstock; 104 (LO), PhotoDisc; 105, John Kelly/Iconica/Getty Images; 106 (CTR), Jim Sugar/Corbis; 106 (LO), Alex Staroseltsev/Shutterstock; 106-107 (UP), jarvis gray/Shutterstock; 107 (UP RT), Steve Raymer/NationalGeographicStock.com; 107 (CTR RT), Jeff Hunter/Photographer's Choice/Getty Images; 108 (UP), Bryan Brazil/Shutterstock; 108 (CTR), Raymond Gehman/NationalGeographicStock.com; 108 (LO), David P. Smith/Shutterstock; 109, Dick Durrance II/NationalGeographicStock.com; 110 (UP), Noah Clayton/The Image Bank/Getty Images; 110 (LO), Doug Lemke/Shutterstock; 111 (LE), Geoffrey Kuchera/Shutterstock; 111 (RT), Jerry Sharp/Shutterstock; 112 (CTR), W. Robert Moore/NationalGeographicStock.com; 112 (LO), Sam Abell/NationalGeographicStock.com; 112-113 (UP), Andy Z./Shutterstock; 113, Danita Delimont/Alamy; 114 (UP), Jennifer Lynn Arnold/Shutterstock; 114 (CTR), Rachell Coe/Shutterstock; 114-115 (LO), Peter Kunasz/Shutterstock; 115 (RT), Tischenko Irina/Shutterstock; 116 (UP), Grafton Marshall Smith/Corbis; 116 (CTR), Nelson Sirlin/Shutterstock; 116 (LO), PhotoDisc; 118 (UP), Natalia Bratslavsky/Shutterstock; 118 (LO), Luis Salazar/Shutterstock; 119 (LE), oksana.perkins/Shutterstock; 119 (RT), Sandy Buckley/Shutterstock; 120 (UP), Videowokart/Shutterstock; 120 (LO), Henryk Sadura/Shutterstock; 121 (LE), Peter Kunasz/Shutterstock; 121 (RT), Nancy Bauer/Shutterstock

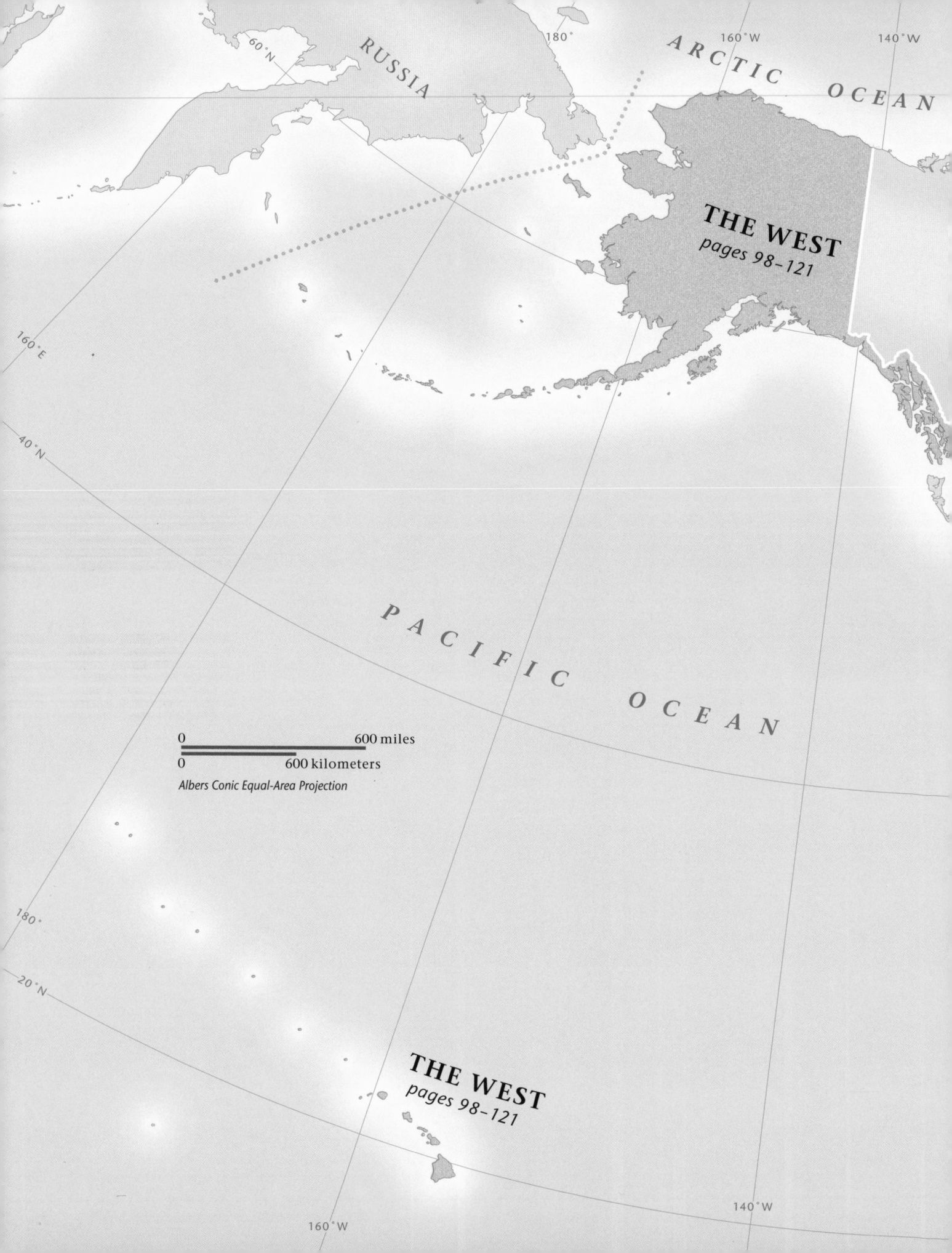
RUSSIA
ARCTIC OCEAN
THE WEST
pages 98–121
PACIFIC OCEAN
0 600 miles
0 600 kilometers
Albers Conic Equal-Area Projection
THE WEST
pages 98–121
60°N
180°
160°W
140°W
160°E
40°N
180°
20°N
160°W
140°W